BUILDERS

BUILDERS

by
Irene M. Franck
and
David M. Brownstone

A Volume in the Work Throughout History Series

A Hudson Group Book

Facts On File Publications
New York, New York ● Oxford, England

11/13 FOL 15⁰⁰ (handwritten)

Builders

0188 YBP LIB 13.95 (handwritten)

Copyright © 1985
by Irene Franck and David Brownstone

Library of Congress Cataloging-in-Publication Data

Franck, Irene M.
   The builders.

11/3 FOL 15⁰⁰ (handwritten)

   (Work throughout history series)
   "A Hudson Group book."
   Bibliography: p.
   Includes index.
   Summary: Explores the role throughout history of the
occupations involved with building, including architects,
contractors, construction laborers, masons, roadbuilders,
and tunnelers.
   1. Building—History—Juvenile literature.
2. Building—Vocational guidance—Juvenile literature.
[1. Building—History. 2. Occupations—History]
I. Brownstone, David M.   II. Title.   III. Series.

TH149.F73 1986   624'.09   85-29175
ISBN 0-8160-1366-7

Printed in the United States of America
10 9 8 7 6 5 4 3 2 1

Contents

Preface

Builders is a book in the multivolume series, *Work Throughout History*. Work shapes the lives of all human beings; yet surprisingly little has been written about the history of the many fascinating and diverse types of occupations men and women pursue. The books in the *Work Throughout History* series explore humanity's most interesting, important, and influential occupations. They explain how and why these occupations came into being in the major cultures of the world, how they evolved over the centuries, especially with changing technology, and how society's view of each occupation has changed. Throughout we focus on what it was like to do a particular kind of work—for example, to be a farmer, glassblower, midwife, banker, building contractor, actor, astrologer, or weaver—in centuries past and right up to today.

Because many occupations have been closely related to one another, we have included at the end of each article references to other overlapping occupations. In preparing this series, we have drawn on a wide range of general works on social, economic, and occupational history, including many on everyday life throughout history. We consulted far too many such wide-ranging works to list them all here; but at the end of each volume is a list of suggestions for further reading, should readers want to learn more about any of the occupations included in the volume.

Many researchers and writers worked on the preparation of this series. For *Builders*, the primary researcher-writer was Thomas Crippen; David Merrill also worked on parts of this volume. Our thanks go to them for their fine work; to our expert typists, Shirley Fenn, Nancy Fishelberg, and Mary Racette; to our most helpful editors at Facts On File, first Kate Kelly and then James Warren, and his assistant Claire Johnston; to our excellent developmental editor, Vicki Tyler; and to our publisher, Edward Knappman, who first suggested the Work Throughout History series and has given us gracious support during the long years of its preparation.

Irene M. Franck
David M. Brownstone

Introduction

The work of builders is all around us. Our homes, schools, offices, churches, bridges, ships, canals, fortresses, and roads have all been created by the people in the building trades. Builders have created not only these everyday structures we live with but also the greatest and most beautiful architectural creations in the world. The pyramids of Egypt, the Great Wall of China, the Parthenon of Greece, the Colosseum of Rome, the Taj Mahal of India, Notre Dame Cathedral of Paris, Westminster Abbey of London, the Empire State Building of New York City, the Golden Gate Bridge of San Francisco, the Panama Canal of Central America, and Columbus's *Nina, Pinta,* and *Santa Maria*—all testify to the skill of builders throughout history.

Whatever the type of building, *construction laborers* are sure to be employed. They do most of the digging, cutting, smoothing, hauling, preparing, and placing of the building materials. For thousands of years their work was done mostly with musclepower, but today—in industrialized countries, at least—many construction workers have powerful machines to aid in this labor. Some construction laborers have always worked as *tunnelers*, especially in underground mines; in the last century the development of explosives has led some people to become specialist *blasters*, able to move large amounts of rock and earth with controlled explosions. The great highways of the Earth—like those of the Roman Empire, the Inca Empire in South America, and the modern countries that rely on automobiles—were constructed by *roadbuilders*.

Overseeing the large building projects of history have been *architects* and *contractors*. In early centuries, architects were often called *building masters*; they learned how to plan buildings primarily through experience over long years of practical construction work. Contractors handled the complex task of assembling the labor and materials needed. Only gradually did architects begin to study formally, particularly in mathematics and engineering, to prepare for their work. For most of history, great structures were built to order; architects were paid to create projects for a specified person or purpose. But in modern times some people—called *contractors*—began to build structures on speculation; they would fund their projects with their own (or borrowed) money, hoping to be able to sell or rent what they built.

Some people in the building trades became specialists in working with certain materials. Those who work with stone, brick, cement, and concrete are known as *masons*. While some masons did the rough work of shaping and placing great stones, others became expert at doing finer work, requiring more accuracy and skill. The masons who built the great cathedrals of Europe, for example, were highly respected artisans, who had considerably more status than *rough masons* or construction laborers.

Carpenters specialize in building with wood. In early times, many carpenters even went into the forest to select the right trees for building, doing or overseeing the actual preparation of the wood personally. Many carpenters throughout history have done rough work; they used cut and shaped, but not sanded-smooth, boards and beams to build their frames or crude buildings. It was left to others to finish the structures built by these *rough carpenters*. Often the finishing was done by specialist carpenters called *joiners*, who did fine, detailed woodworking, such as that required for stairs, windows, and doors.

Other *finishing workers* were also employed. *Plasterers* often finished the walls and ceiling, sometimes the outside as well, by applying a layer of a paste-like mixture called *plaster*. Beautiful pictures called *frescoes* were sometimes painted on the hardened plaster surfaces, but it was not until recent centuries that large numbers of *house painters* and *paperhangers* were employed to finish the inner and outer walls of buildings. Some building workers specialized in working on certain parts of a structure. *Paviors* created beautifully designed floors from specially shaped pieces of wood, stone, or other materials. *Roofers* applied materials like slate or matted reeds atop the building to protect the inside from rain, sun, and snow. *Glaziers* installed windows, large and small. In modern times, most buildings—at least in industrialized countries—are built with running water. So a new group of specialists—*plumbers*—took on the work of installing the systems that bring water to where it is needed and carry away the waste.

In a class all their own were the *shipwrights*. In addition to their skill in working with wood—or whatever other materials might be used for a boat—they had to know how to design the boat so that it held its crew and cargo afloat in safety; how to fit the parts of the boat together so that it could stand pounding by waves, currents, and storms; and how to seal the outer skin of the craft against leaks of water, which could sink the ship. From the days of the Phoenicians and Greeks through the great eras of Moslem and Italian sailing to the age of modern navies, shipwrights with the right combination of skills have always been valued artisans.

Architects and Contractors

Architects and *contractors* are the people responsible not for the physical work of erecting a building, but for conceiving of the building in the first place and then supervising its progress until it is completed. In modern times the architect plans a building, while the building contractor assembles the needed workers and their materials. However, the two jobs often overlap, and throughout history they have often been the responsibility of a single professional.

Ancient Egypt's *building masters* were as much contractors as architects. Contracting—that is, assembling workers and materials—was a relatively easy job for them. Because they built for pharaohs (rulers) and the other nobles of Egypt, the building masters could simply requisition whatever number of laborers and whatever

Architects supervising major construction, such as this Babylonian ziggurat, *had extraordinarily high status in their countries. (From Diderot's* Encyclopedia, *late 18th century)*

amount of stone they wished. As the pharaoh's lieutenant, the building master decided what the building would look like and administered all the materials that had been collected for the building.

These early Egyptian building masters were powerful people. They had won charge of something very important to the pharaoh: his own glorification. It took thousands of laborers working with millions of tons of stone to make one pyramid; these all rested under the architect's control. The first of Egypt's architects, so far as is known, was Imhotep. He designed the first pyramid, built in rising levels of steps; 2850 B.C. is the date traditionally given for its completion. Imhotep had not been born to one of Egypt's important families, but his drive and talent carried him very far; among the official titles he chose before his death were "Chancellor of the King of Lower Egypt, Chief under the King of Upper Egypt, Administrator of the Great Mansion"; he was also a physician worshipped long after his death.

Looking after all the goods the pharaoh had collected meant being on the site where they were used, and making sure the workers did their jobs and the project went forward. That is why another Egyptian architect, in his epitaph, was proud to describe himself as "foreman of foremen." The Egyptian word for *architect* translates as "master of the builders" or "overseer of works." In planning buildings, an architect had to guess at the ways blocks and masses would relate to one another; rules of thumb counted more than calculation, for no one at the time knew much about higher mathematics.

The rules of thumb had to be learned, of course, and architects were given professional training by the day's educators, the *priests*. One man began his education at age five, spent 12 years in study, and then worked his way up in the religious hierarchy, finishing his life as court architect and the second prophet to Amun. He may well have been a newcomer to the profession; other men, once winning expertise, passed it on within the family. Father-and-son lines of architects became a tradition. One lasted 25 generations, into the fifth century B.C. Throughout the history of architecture, families have often tried to keep the profession for themselves alone.

In ancient Egypt, all designs for the pharaoh's buildings were drawn on sheets of papyrus or leather and stored away in the palace archives; these plans could be brought out for future remodeling. The goddess Seshat, Lady of Builders and Writing, was believed to preside over the archives. It is not clear whether the architect drew the plans before or after raising a building.

For the first day of work, a *plan-net*, a system of cords, was stretched over the building site and pulled taut along the estimated length of the project. By stretching out the appropriate number of cords, the architect could calculate the width of the building. Seshat was invoked in a ritual with the pharaoh presiding; then a *priest* read from the *Book of Foundations*, a basic text of the profession, thought (like most early writings) to have dropped from the skies. After that, building could proceed by simple geometry and the architect's practical expertise.

Across the Mediterranean, in Greece and then Rome, builders were producing great buildings—what we now call Classical architecture— in the thousand years before Christ, and continued into the fifth century A.D. Greco-Roman architects worked as independent professionals, rather than officers of the state, but most building was still conceived of and paid for by the government. In the late sixth century B.C., when the Greek temple at Delphi had to be rebuilt, the city's council chose the architect and contracted for the supply of limestone and marble. Similarly, in Rome, the officers of the Senate, who were called *censors*, took charge of the vast public building works under the Republic. In later years, the Roman emperor appointed his own lieutenants to serve as civic contractors. The architect thus became a design specialist, hired for his talents to plan buildings and supervise their construction, but without expectation of any power in the state.

The Duke of Chou is shown here urging on the artisans under his supervision. (From Chhin-Ting Shu Ching Thu Shuo, *imperial illustrated edition of the* Historical Classic, *1905)*

The Greek word *architekton* means *supreme* or *master carpenter*; chief builders shared this title with *shipwrights*. The title *supreme carpenter* did not mean, however, that the architect was merely a carpenter who had risen to the top of his craft. Rather, it meant that the *architekton* was supreme among those working on a project, being the guiding mind on a building team. A small private home might be built solely through the craft of the *masons* and *carpenters* who raised it; planning such a structure was as much a part of their traditions as sawing wood or laying brick on brick. But no ordinary carpenter or mason could comprehend the raising of military fortifications or a temple. That took a person who could think through an entire complicated project and then coordinate all the workers needed for the task. The Greek architekton was the first individual to take on this enormous job alone. The Romans later adopted the ideas of the architektons, as well as their name, which appears as *architect* in medieval manuscripts and continues with us today.

No paper sketches or designs by the Classical architects have survived. Tradition has it that they worked out their ideas in models, using moldable wax for alterations. Both Greeks and Romans drew up specifications, that is, lists of a proposed building's dimensions and the workers and materials required for its construction. Each day the architect posted orders for workers on the site.

The Classical architects took charge of anything too complicated for a group of workers to handle by themselves. This is why Greek shipwrights and architects shared the same title—the shipwright was an architect who planned and oversaw the construction of ships. An architect understood how any great structure could be raised, whether it was a villa, a statue, a lighthouse, a city's system of sewers, or a city itself. Architects set sail with the Greek colonists, to plan the new homes they built throughout the Mediterranean.

The first centuries of the Roman Empire saw a great age for *civil engineers*, though they had not yet acquired that name. Civil engineers specialize in the design and construction of highways, bridges, tunnels, waterworks, and harbors. When the Roman state began its great work of building around the Mediterranean, it required architects who could design and oversee the construction of roads, aqueducts, and port facilities. The government employed its own league of architects, each one assigned as a civil servant to one department or another. Some worked on roads, others aqueducts, and so on. Architects traveled with Rome's armies, to guide them in constructing military fortifications; Hadrian's Wall, built across the neck of Britain, was one of their notable achievements.

Until the Classical period, architecture had developed very slowly, but the Greeks made enormous advances in a relatively short period. Its practitioners learned to construct buildings that, 2,000 years later, are still thought of as masterpieces. Structures like the Parthenon in Athens showed that architecture could be counted as both a science and an art, for in producing these beautiful buildings Classical architects drew more on higher mathematics than any architects had done before. A treasury built for the city of Cyrene in the fourth century B.C. was founded on proportions making use of square roots.

Greek architects had learned their craft on the job, finding their way around building sites the way a novice in another craft might spend years in a workshop. The Roman architects who followed them, however, received more formal training. Apprentices assisted established practitioners; the master architect, in return, made sure that the by-then extensive fundamentals of the profession were passed on. Roman architects took seriously all the secrets at their command. Nikodemus inscribed on one building, erected in the second century A.D., that "solid and plane geometry" alone made possible the understanding of construction, and also of the world.

Greek architects, in their science and their demands upon themselves, were at least the match of any professional architect of today. This fact makes the question of their status, the attention society paid them, rather puzzling. The status of architects varied widely. Some were highly regarded members of the community. Others, most of them Greeks taken to Rome, were actually slaves. Carpenters, *sawyers*, even people who built a project's scaffolds, could earn as much as did the architect directing them. Sometimes the architect earned far more; sometimes the architect's recorded wages were rather less.

Greek architects seem to have taken on much of their work as a civic duty. Architects wanted honor and took their fees as a token, much as retired public servants of today might accept a dollar a year for teaching at a university.

However, no profession could last if its members worked only for honor. The architects had to support themselves. Among the Romans, where great lords rivaled the state in their building, architects charged fees and could collect substantial fortunes. Even centuries before, in Greece, many architects had gone about landing projects in a way that, if the object was honor, seems single-minded. On the one hand were architects such as Libon of Elis, who built the magnificent Temple of Zeus at Olympia and then retired; in this case, the architect was satisfied with the honor he had won. On the other hand were architects such as Christophus of Crete, who toured Greece's outlying city-states, collecting commissions. In his practice he showed the thoroughness of a businessman, someone determined to make a good living by finding as much work as possible. Still, his fees were not very high, and he was not a rich man. Greek *painters* and *sculptors* sometimes made fortunes; architects did not.

Many architects did earn a great deal of honor, however. In the fifth century B.C., the architects of Athens, under the direction of the statesman and general Pericles, were cheered by crowds when speaking in praise of their own work. Pericles himself is said to have studied architecture with Anaxagoras, one of his closest friends. Roman architects won even more acclaim. Some even served in the Senate. Building inscriptions named the designer, even when they might ignore the patrons who had paid for the building. The Temple of Cyzicus, commissioned by the Emperor Hadrian (whose admirers claimed for him an expert's standing in architecture), bears an inscription that reads: "From the foundations, with money from all of Asia, and with the help of many hands, the god-like Aristainetos raised me up." Aristainetos, of course, was the architect hired by his emperor to design the temple.

Classical architects conducted themselves as a class of learned *scholars*. They expounded upon their art; and their debates, in and out of print, were signs of the endless thinking that made possible subtlety and innovation. Books on architecture began to appear in the fourth century B.C.; they discussed not only structure, but the aesthetics of building, what kind of designs were most pleasing to look at. Architects explored in print almost every aspect of their work.

The best-remembered of the Roman architects was a patrician, or nobleman, named Vitruvius. His skills may have been mediocre; in fact, he may have done little designing at all. His major achievement was that he wrote about the profession in 10 volumes, which are invaluable historical references for us today. Vitruvius wanted to present architecture to the educated reader, from mathematical theory to ways of grouping houses and supplying water. His Greek sources are listed exhaustively. Once written down in full this way, architecture had a better chance of survival; the volumes were preserved through Europe's Dark Ages, and remained the final word on architecture for long afterward, up to the 18th century.

His readers were not surprised that the aristocratic Vitruvius should have chosen architecture for his life work. Architecture had become a genteel pursuit. In earlier centuries, one of the Republic's great statesmen might casually describe an argument over the design of his new villa, an argument which he would lose to the architect, one of his slaves. But by the late Roman

Empire, educated gentlemen claimed architecture for themselves. *Architectus*, as the name of a profession, had become passé: the term came to mean any person who claimed to be a builder but had not been educated in theory. In 334 A.D., when the Emperor Constantine decided to build a new capital (which would be named Constantinople after him), he found that not enough builders of skill remained in the Empire to carry out his orders. To train more builders, he founded a system of state schools, where architects chosen by the state could pass on their skills. A student would enter school in early manhood to be qualified as a *mechanicus*, or a builder with an understanding of his art.

For centuries, the Mediterranean's great building was done in Constantinople (formerly called Byzantium). When Rome and the Western Empire collapsed as a result of the barbarian conquests of the fifth century A.D., Constantinople drew the wealth of Rome's remaining provinces to itself. One of the great Byzantine buildings

With the medieval intertwining of architecture and religion, it was easy to see God as an architect. (Austrian National Library, Vienna)

erected during this period was an immense domed church called Hagia Sophia, finished in 537 A.D. A building of this scale had not been seen since the early Roman Empire. The Emperor Justinian commissioned it from two men, Anthemius and Isidorus, who had learned architecture as scholars rather than as *master-builders*. The church was built of brick, held together by a cement-like mixture called mortar. The stresses of the dome's weight worked down, as a chronicler put it, "like active demons." The architects sent the weight upward again with a system of half-domes and buttresses, structural supports reinforcing whatever seemed weak in the structure. Their ambitions ran very high and strained many a tried-and-true engineering law; in the end, the building collapsed, pulling apart during an earthquake in 558 A.D. The nephew of one of the original architects later rebuilt the church. The dome rose 20 feet higher and rested on broader supports. Hagia Sophia was reconsecrated in 563, and still stands.

Constantinople's neighbors in the Middle East were Moslems, who had emerged out of Arabia with their new Islamic religion in the eighth century A.D. The rulers of the Islamic nations enjoyed the old practice of building in their own honor. The kings of impoverished medieval Europe could not have imagined the palaces the *caliphs* and *sultans* commanded for themselves. The structures were airy and elaborate, their surfaces filled out with glass windows and painted tiles. They required skill from their builders, but only an occasional Moslem *mathematician*, who had tried something new, is remembered by name. No schools taught architectural theory; in fact, very little theory was used. Architects graduated from advanced handwork in such crafts as pottery or glassworking. The Islamic title for architect is often translated as "Master," but is actually somewhat closer to "Competent to Build". The architect of one mosque (an Islamic house of worship) was paid the same as the *marbler* who worked beneath him; they both earned less than the gatekeeper.

Moslem architects lived in cities, working for caliphs and nobles. These patrons could be extremely capricious and cruel. Hasan, sultan of Cairo, so admired a new mosque that—the tale goes—he had the hands of its designer sliced off because he wanted to make sure the building would not be duplicated.

In countries such as China and Japan, on the other hand, building was an orderly process administered primarily by the government. Efficiency counted. Government officials contracted for workers, tools, and goods; *designers* labored for an impersonal state. A modern architectural observer has noted: "Chinese buildings, for all the sophisticated aesthetic that controls every part, have a look of being built by a master-craftsman or architect-engineer, as indeed they were." Carpenters managed most private building, which was generally of wood; and master-carpenters and masons also did the practical day-to-day supervision of large public construction, which involved a wider range of materials. The government architects in the Directorate of Building and Construction were essentially what we today would call "white-collar" workers, more scholars than artisans, whose knowledge came largely from collections of technical manuals on the art of building.

Chinese architects made drawings and miniature models of the projects they were building; these included the surrounding terrain, for these experts were also *landscape architects*, not simply building specialists. Their tradition of designing gardens and parks much influenced other East Asian countries, and predated by centuries the modern landscape architecture movements in the West.

Japan drew much from China. Buddhist temples in seventh-century Japan were built by the state, beginning with the founding of the government's Yakushi-ji Construction Agency by the architect Temmu. The Kofuku-ji Construction Agency followed in 720 A.D. Each had a specific sphere of projects assigned to it. A Japanese monk named Chogen traveled throughout China in the 12th century, returning with methods for the quick raising of buildings by specialized work teams; for this contribution, he is remembered by the Japanese as "the Great Architect."

Indian architects were neither as formal nor as organized. Rather than focusing on logical, geometrical constructions, they stressed the religious unity of the building with both gods and humans. Architectural historian Talbot Hamlin noted: "...for the Hindu architect counts no cost too great, no extravagance too excessive, if thereby more of this almost hypnotic identification can be achieved. Thus we get endless repetitions of molding on molding, form on form, and sculptural decoration so enormous in quantity as to defy all but the most patient analysis." The somewhat simpler Buddhist architecture of India, drawing on Greek styles, spread eastward across Central Asia, and much influenced Chinese and Japanese architects. In turn, India's architects were influenced by the Moslem architectural tradition, which gradually spread to the subcontinent from the Near East. Indeed, the various architectures of Central and Western Asia became increasingly intertwined; many Moslem buildings were constructed on foundations laid by previous cultures.

The Ottoman Turks overwhelmed the Near East in the 15th century, becoming the last of the region's great Islamic empires. Their building surpassed that of their predecessors; architects became some of the realm's most famous citizens. Constantinople, eventually renamed Istanbul, was the home of a famous group of mosques, all built in patterns of dark and light stone. The finest of these mosques was thought to be the one built by Sinan. It made him a celebrity from the day it was completed.

Sinan had begun as a construction worker; conscripted by the army and set to work on military fortifications, he showed that he understood their design better than any of his officers did. The military advanced Sinan rapidly and, by the time he was discharged, his skills had been established. A lieutenant of Suleiman the Magnificent, ruler of the Ottoman Empire in the mid-16th century, Sinan trained a school of students; and kings from around the Islamic world—even as far away as India—competed for the services of those students. The Sultan's forest tracts were placed under Sinan's supervision; he set aside wood for building, having it cut to the dimensions he required. With the throne's money, Sinan began a surge of building that lasted through the next century and set the pattern for the Islamic world into modern times.

While architecture was flourishing in the East, the West was in a deep decline. Under the barbarian kingdoms that occupied former Roman lands, the Classical legacy was largely lost. As a science, architecture vanished. Through the Dark Ages, from the fifth to the tenth century, most building was begun and finished by work teams under their foremen. Only rarely did a few signs of more advanced planning appear. Northern Italy's kings in the seventh and eighth centuries recognized organizations of *master-builders*: the *associated masons*. Primitive sorts of specifications and blueprints, designs of a building's structure, have been discovered from the eighth century. Monasteries preserved copies of the Roman noble Vitruvius's writings on architecture, copying them for posterity. The Abbot of St. Gall, an enterprising man, devised a scale model with which he could guide the rebuilding of his monastery. An early portrait of a person who may have been an architect dates from 775 A.D.: a wall painting in France's church of St.-Denis portrays a monk looking up to heaven, a small-scale church in his hands. By the 10th century, Westminster Abbey's builder, Godwin Gretsyd, earned enough from his work to leave legacies of land and money to Winchester's Hyde Abbey. Even so, it was six centuries after the fall of Rome before stone-building gave a class of specialists anything like regular employment.

The knowledge and skills that had been lost had to be rediscovered; however, few people had the opportunity or training for inventive thinking. Perhaps more to the point, medieval builders could relearn their trade only

Cathedral-builders really did hold their constructions in the palms of their hands, for no one else could see the whole before it was finished. (By Albrecht Dürer, early 16th century)

when they had the chance to build. The Normans of 11th-century France and England built with scale and ambitions that they had learned from their Arab enemies. What they did not have, however, was the Arabs' understanding of building. Great Norman towers, once raised, often fell down. Builders during this *Romanesque* period could only pile stone in thick-walled, wide-based structures, for any divergence might lead to an unstable building. From the end of the 11th century onward, however, European builders began to create more graceful, tapered structures that reached higher and with more delicate calculation into the air. For the next two centuries, this *Gothic* style—probably spread by travelling French master-masons—was the only kind of ambitious building that could be found in Europe; it remained a model into the 20th century.

Masons raised the medieval buildings from stone; the man who directed each enterprise was also a mason. This

These architectural workers are delineating the proper ellipse for an arch in their construction. (From Bachot's Le Gouvernail, *1598)*

master-mason stood apart from those who carried out his commands. For a building to stand, its builder had to know how stone could be used; the master-mason had to have intelligence and the ability to command other people. The master-mason was also called a *master of works* or *ingeniator* (experience in building military fortifications was included in that title).

The master of a Gothic building prepared his plans, including the structure of the edifice and the materials required, and then displayed them to his patrons for approval. Structural plans, some of them drawn with great skill, date from the 13th century; tracings on stone floor slabs have been discovered from earlier periods.

Until the 11th century, many of the masters were *priests* or *monks*. The Catholic church launched great enterprises in building, and church libraries preserved what was left of the old science. Even after laymen took on building—first in Italy and then in 12th-century France and England—the monasteries continued to teach the principles of architecture. Some of the lay masters learned their trade there; more worked and learned on their own, as masons.

Precise measurement became universal during the Gothic period, as builders mastered it for designing plans, marking out plots of land, preparing sites, checking the delivery of materials, and judging the accuracy of craftsmen's work. Builders had to understand proportion and geometry. They could not have practiced without knowing how to trace a right angle on the ground, calculate the size of foundations, and then mark out the site with pegs and cord. At first geometry translated into rules of thumb, a list of basic relationships that the builder memorized. As buttresses and flying vaults became more involved, the builders' mathematics became more sophisticated: their geometry approached the level we know today.

Lords and kings commanded stone castles, which were necessary at a time when wars were frequent. But the greatest of the medieval buildings were the cathedrals. The church built on a grand scale, raising inspirational Gothic arches, rather than simple walls thick enough for protection. Once vaulting—the building of peaked roofs so that their stones support one another—had been mastered, churches and cathedrals could expand in all directions. Cathedrals climbed heights and spread over acres of ground. With vaulting, the choir of St. Peter's cathedral at Beauvais, France reached a height of 150 feet.

Carpenters, masons, plumbers, glaziers, plasterers, tilers, smiths, roofers, and a large number of construction laborers would all work together on the same site. The unskilled lifters and pushers could be gathered from among the local peasants; some skilled jobs, if not too complex, could be performed by serfs used to keeping their master's castle in repair. But the highly skilled workers who made a project possible were not as easy to obtain. The master had to find them, size them up, bargain with them, and then keep them steadily doing their best work. He also dispensed their pay, their materials, and sometimes even their tools.

The master received money and materials from his patrons. The patrons who had chosen him also chose the materials of his work. The master's patron might be a bishop of the church, who would decide on a building project and then divert enough of the church's wealth to launch it. Bishop Suger, for example, began the rebuilding of France's church of St.-Denis upon being made abbot; he made sure he had the best of workers and goods, stipulated designs, and saw that his name was listed in each of the church's stone inscriptions.

A nobleman building his palace had a *steward* directing finances; a king had a finance minister for the same job. A bishop would appoint a lower-ranking churchman to oversee the financial operations of the building project and an office of priests supplied the materials for the building and inspected the use made of them. The builder had to answer to these and other people.

Gathering the materials for a project was done in ways different from those of today. It was an age of power rather than of money. Anyone eminent enough to build a castle or a cathedral could expect deference from the rest of his society—some demanded it. To build their castles, Europe's kings kidnapped work gangs. Churchmen did not have to be so forceful. By tradition, worshippers gave a tithe—that is, a tenth of their income—to the church every year. Thus, a bishop with a cathedral to be built could easily find a variety of religious-minded donors to provide stone quarries, serfs, brickyards, and a fleet of carts as well. With good fortune, the cleric might need to supply only a master-builder and a few skilled workers.

For less fortunate patrons, a master-builder might try his hand as a *contractor*, relying on his contacts among *quarry-owners* and *timber-cutters*. Surviving contracts indicate that contracting of this sort may also have been taken on by common laboring masons who had some ambition.

The patron, having assembled necessities, bound the master-builder by contract. No guilds or royal rules determined these agreements; the builder bargained on his own for the best contract he could get and then delivered his talents. Payment varied widely. Some builders made fortunes; Eudes de Monteneau, builder to the 13th-century French court, earned each year—with combined salary and favors—approximately the equivalent of $10,000. But a master-mason in England might expect 18 pence in a day, three times what one of his chief working masons would earn.

Real wealth, however, belonged only to the masters of society: the kings, the lords, and the church. It was not about to shift to the workers' hands. The reward for outstanding work was usually a bit of privilege. Security and social position are what a builder looked for in a contract; for centuries, these were what he negotiated for when settling terms. A patron contracted a builder's services for a certain number of years or for life, and the builder was glad of it. The contract set his pay; it set when he might leave for other projects and how long he might stay away; sometimes the contract even spelled out what the builder could or could not do with his free time. Health insurance, half-pay for old age, and a house to live in might all be included in a contract.

The builder gave his talents, and he often received a good deal in return for them. Special privileges often came his way; he might be excused from paying taxes, for example. The master-mason of England's York Cathedral was paid even while away from work. The privilege of wearing furred robes showed that successful builders belonged to the rank of esquires, in effect, junior members of the aristocracy. Eudes de Montreuil, for example, was a friend, as well as employee, of France's Louis IX, traveling with him on a Crusade and overseeing a building in the Holy Land. Tomb slabs and other monuments, carved with great lavishness, mark the graves of numerous builders who had won their way in the world. The castles and cathedrals they erected came, more and more often, to bear the builder's name, inscribed in the walls. The more ambitious builders even had likenesses of themselves carved into the stone of the building.

Building masters could read and write in both Latin and their native tongues. Richard of Wolverston, a 12th-century builder, collected letters that had been painted and illuminated; he was more cultivated than any of the age's nobility. Medieval building plans, growing in number from the 13th century, were executed with an accomplished attention to detail that indicates a learned tradition behind them. Each building site had a *drawing office* attached to the masons' lodge. The more talented builders grew restless working for one master at a time, when their services were being sought by so many others. Shuttling from project to project, they drew their ideas on paper, and then left a deputy to command the work site.

Some of the most famous early architectural drawings are those of Villard de Honnecourt, dating from the early 13th century. He drew gargoyles and pillars, details of stone-setting, elevations (a building seen face on), and structural plans. All these came from cathedrals and palaces across Northern Europe, to which de Honnecourt had traveled for ideas. De Honnecourt's drawings reflect an important feature of many contracts for builders in the late Middle Ages: a chance to go off and search out the new developments of their art.

Builders knew one another; a good one could be famous for hundreds of miles, an extensive radius in those times. A board of builders might be convened from great distances to give advice on some stubborn problem of structure. De Honnecourt's album may have been designed for sharing with a group of other builders, as a report on new techniques. The album is filled with finished drawings, not sketches, and each one is accompanied by a small essay. It had once again become professional practice to find or produce new ideas, and a community of builders carried these ideas through Western Europe.

By the end of the 15th century, builders were recognized as men who made their livings by designing buildings; architecture had reappeared. Builders first gave way to designers in Italy. The wealth of its cities had nurtured the great revival of culture we call the Renaissance. Filippo Brunelleschi is credited as the first great artist of Italian architecture. Tradition says that he was the first to demonstrate the difference between an *architect* and a *builder*. While working on the Florence cathedral with a troublesome master-mason in 1423, Brunelleschi pretended illness one day and let his lieutenant take over; the man soon came to his sickbed, asking for instructions. Thus, Brunelleschi demonstrated how indispensable the designer of a building had become. The builder could no longer function without him.

Brunelleschi's great inspiration came when, as a young man, he visited Rome. The ruins of the Classical builders' work still stood; the new architects, a good thousand years later, looked on them with awe. Almost every man whom Giacomo Vasari, biographer of Renaissance artists, described as an architect had managed to settle for a time in Rome. Brunelleschi worked as a *jeweler*, setting gems, to support himself in the great city. Another architect measured Rome's ancient buildings for 12 years, working part-time as a painter's assistant.

Some in the trade were trained by working as architects' assistants; sons or younger brothers in the great architectural families were favored for this, of course. But of the architects whose lives were described by Vasari, only four were sons of architects. Three were sons of painters; three were nobles; two others noble but impoverished; six were sons of laborers. Their fathers had planned other vocations for their sons—*notary*, *lawyer*, *weaver*—but the young men made themselves architects. In a profession as complex as architecture, this took some determination.

A poor boy had to hope that some rich noble would see promise in him and provide the necessary training. For most, education in school came first. Signs of artistic talent could bring the boy an apprenticeship with a painter or sculptor. Only one female architect is mentioned, fleetingly, from this time, as an entrant in a competition against Brunelleschi.

Some artists of the Renaissance mastered many art forms. Michelangelo, the great painter and sculptor, was also a great architect; Leonardo da Vinci drew designs for military engines. It was not so unlikely that an apprentice to a painter could, when independent, take up architecture as his career. *Goldsmiths* and *sculptors* trained the largest share of future builders. When architects directed *painters* and *sculptors* in the decoration of buildings, they often joined in the work themselves; throughout their careers, the architects remained highly skilled craftsmen as well as designers of buildings.

An architectural hopeful had years of work before him. On his own or under a teacher, he had to master the rules and traditions of a profession yearly becoming more scientific; much of this learning was done during the years architects spent examining Rome's buildings. Bartolommeo Genga, who had something of a head start

When Europeans spread around the world, they generally had their own architects build houses abroad, using local laborers. (From The New America and the Far East, by G. Waldo Browne, 1901)

as the apprentice of his architect father, was not ready to work as an architect until the age of 28.

The architect was one of Renaissance Italy's most highly regarded craftsmen, ranked with the sculptor and the painter. Good work brought high pay, as well as state honors, positions, and pensions. These could be much more impressive than anything the medieval master-masons had gained. In the 16th century, the great architects associated with the most powerful men of the age. Vasari, an architect himself, worked on the Roman palace of Cardinal Farnese and was regularly invited to dinner with the Cardinal's noble guests. Renaissance architects were often touchy, pampered geniuses, who freely insulted their patrons and made eccentric demands, which were often treated with respect. The architect Verrocchio, Vasari tells us, had it in his contract that "the door of...wherever he was kept, should be left constantly open."

Living among the great, architects found work through their social connections, sponsors in the nobility, and the upper reaches of church and state. Competitions for a project pitted architects' ideas against each other, but the competitions were open only to those invited. Architects even designed dramatic entertainments called *masques*—which featured elaborate scenery and costumes—for their patrons. Devising such entertainment was part of their profession, and many architects took pride in it.

By the 17th century, the designers of Italy's buildings and forts had become specialists; a man who painted, set gems, or sculpted could no longer be expected to oversee the raising of a tower. An architect did not peddle his talents from court to court; instead, he maintained a private practice, and clients came to him. Pay climbed still higher, though it is unclear whether a salary bought up a block of an architect's time or left him free for other projects. Training was still by apprenticeship and then study in Rome. A boy might begin to prepare for the profession at age 12, and his education would include mathematics, geometry, mechanical logic, and perspective. In 1577, Rome's Academy of St. Luke was reorganized as the center of a literary and artistic community. It began formal training in architecture, as well as in painting and sculpture. Academies in other Italian cities followed, through the 18th century.

Architects belonged to Italy's very small but affluent upper middle class. A craftsman's son could still work his way into the profession, but most of his colleagues would belong to families of *lawyers*, *scholars*, and *artists*. Architects sometimes won great popular acclaim. When Domenico Fontana erected an ancient obelisk in Rome, he was carried on the shoulders of an enthusiastic crowd; the obelisk had been left from the days of the Empire and had long been thought too heavy for engineers to once again set upright. Fontana was eventually awarded the honor of Knight of the Golden Spur. A volume written about his triumph over the obelisk was sold all over Europe.

By the late Renaissance, architects were writing down their theories and rules; books of architectural engravings, done by first-rate draftsmen, became standard. The rest of Europe used these Italian books for its education. Italian architects also traveled abroad, invited to foreign courts from Portugal to Austria. The grandest foreign patrons had been able to command Italian architects since the height of the Renaissance. Fontainebleau, the French royal palace, had an Italian architect put in charge of its construction in 1541. The new science was something heard of even in England, where few people had yet learned to master it. Two English officials, writing each other in 1596 over standards for a royal surveyor, discussed whether candidates should "be put on trial...in the rules of architecture, or shipbuilding,....house building, or any such ingenious cause."

The English and French master-masons did not vanish as readily as their colleagues in Italy. However, architects, transplanted or native-born, began to emerge as distinct professionals. The few French architects could earn enviable fees as early as the 16th century. Young men trained for the profession in family firms and were then sent to Rome to perfect their skills. French architects worked from large-scale models of their projects and wrote detailed specifications for them. The specifications for Fontainebleau, written in 1528, ran to 16,500 words; they listed room sizes and numbers, materials to be used, the thickness of chamber walls, and other details of the planned construction.

French power mounted in the 17th century, and the nation's rulers began building in earnest. Cardinal Richelieu, for years the power behind the nation's throne, built a castle—with an accompanying town to house the servants. The French throne dispensed great wealth, and rivalries sprang up over who would direct this wealth, and into whose hands. The pay of a successful architect, often supplemented by bribes from quarry-masters and trade guilds, could be astronomical; J. A. Gabriel earned 20,000 francs per year, close to $200,000 in present-day dollars.

France's Academy of Architecture was founded in 1671 by Louis XIV's minister, Colbert, as part of the *Ecole des Beaux Arts* (School of Fine Arts). Its members, respected architects, met each week as a sort of brain trust for the science. They trained students and set out ranks of merit for members of the profession. Their program introduced students first to theory, then to a practical understanding of aims and materials; Western training in architecture followed this sequence for centuries.

Libraries of architectural designs also grew up. J. H. Mansart hired a large staff of *draftsmen* to represent and fill out his ideas; many went on to building careers of their own. The French began publishing to match the Italians; one book contained 780 detailed engravings. The makers of the books might have been architects themselves; but draftsmanship had come to be so important to its father profession that it could promise tempting prestige and rewards of its own.

The word *architect* first appeared on the title page of an English book, published in 1563. An English architect of

While contractors and visitors supervise, workers assemble the Statue of Liberty from the parts sent from France. (From Frank Leslie's October 17, 1885)

genius, Inigo Jones, was born 10 years later, but he had few fellow architects in his homeland. Master-masons, who had advanced little and sometimes even regressed, since the Middle Ages, still remained in great numbers. Present-day students of architecture have often been puzzled by English houses of the day and their variations from preserved plans. The explanation is simple: inspirations would come to the masons while at work, and they would follow these, rather than what the designer had had in mind. Professional design of buildings and certainty of execution became commonplace among the English only during the 18th century. *Joiners*, experts at interior carpentry, could become architects—Inigo Jones himself had been a joiner's apprentice—but nobles also practiced the art of architecture. Those with a genuine aptitude made a point of designing their own homes; it was one of the accomplishments a well-bred man liked to master, just as his wife and daughter would learn to play the piano for guests.

Well into the 18th century, when English architects had become wealthy and respected men, the limits of the profession were still undefined and in flux. Many men who worked as architects had begun as carpenters, for example, and were called, with full due given to their accomplishments, *master-carpenters*. The word *architect* itself took time to emerge as dominant. *Architectist, architector, architecture,* and *architectur* were all synonyms. *Architecturalist*—more an appreciator than a practitioner of the art—survived into the Victorian Age.

No one had yet agreed on exactly how an architect should be trained. Travel to Rome: that was necessary. Beyond this, it seemed anyone with experience in putting up walls could claim to be a designer. In an advertisement appearing in a newspaper in 1753, Robert Bretingham announced that he was "leaving off his business as a Mason, he intends to act in the character of an Architect, in drawing plans,...giving estimates...or measuring up any sort of building, for any gentleman in the Country."

For thousands of years the person who built a mansion built whatever other great structures the state might require. But with improved technology and a slowly growing fund of capital more structures were being built that were not intended as housing. The profession of the civil engineer began to emerge and flourish, separating itself from that of the architect. Civil engineers first specialized in designing the structures involved in the transport of goods and people over long distances. These included roads, bridges, canals, lighthouses, docks, warehouses, and harbors. Later on into the 20th century, their work would expand to include whatever is needed for the supply of gas and electric energy, the building of airports, and such great complexes as dams, plants for chemical processing, public sewer systems, and water supply systems.

In the late 17th century, the French Academy of Architecture introduced courses on the engineering of roads, canals, fortifications, and bridges. A Bridges and Highways Corps was founded in 1716; a Bridges and Highways School followed in 1747. The rest of Europe learned from France's writers and teachers.

In the field of civil engineering, the English learned quickly. The wealth of the nation was swelling as entrepreneurs found ways to expand trade: the easier transportation could be made, the more could be produced and sold. A variety of craftspeople made their way into the civil engineering profession. James Brindley, England's foremost canal-builder, had been trained as a *millwright*. John Smeaton was the first man to call himself a *civil engineer*. He began as a *scientific instrument-maker*, doing complex work but on a very small scale. Later he designed lighthouses, watermills, and windmills. Gleaned from years of experience, his understanding of materials and methods made him the profession's leader. He gathered the British engineers into their first trade association, the Society of Civil Engineers. Known informally as the *Smeatonian Society*, it worked as a pressure group for more public building. Between 1800 and 1810, 30 acres of docks were built in England. By 1815, a network of canals traveled for 2,600 miles; another 500 miles of canals ran in Ireland and Scotland.

In 1794 the Paris Polytechnical School was founded; 1799 saw a Berlin Polytechnical. The British founded their Institution of Civil Engineers in 1818, training "young men" in "Mechanical Science." Academies and societies followed in the rest of Europe for the next few decades. The first in the United States, the Rensselaer Polytechnic Institute, was founded in 1824. Engineering came to be taught as a respectable branch of higher education. Queen Victoria founded a chair (a permanent allowance for a line of professors) of civil engineering at the University of Glasgow in 1840.

England built to keep pace with its emerging industrial life. Designing public buildings that had not been imagined before—great railway stations and office buildings—provided more work for architects than constructing private mansions had done in the past. The clergy wanted churches. The government and business wanted towers, banks, and hospitals. What had happened in 17th-century Italy now happened in England. Architects gained a new respect and independence as a result of an increasing need and appreciation of the service they provided. The architect's office was the heart of an independent firm; people who a century before would have been patrons were now *clients*. The Government Board of Works gave out commissions to a chosen group of private practices. Most architects had their own firms, perhaps taking on a partner. A few grew beyond this. Sir Gilbert Scott employed a staff so large that he could not recognize many buildings designed under his name. The count of his finished projects comes close to a thousand.

In the early 19th century, building workers made up 6 percent of England's labor force. Among these were *building contractors*, who built on commission, and speculative builders, who built at their own risk, selling the finished structures to later buyers. England's population was still growing, and not many of its members could afford a private home designed by Sir Gilbert Scott. The speculative builder had appeared on the scene in the late 17th century, after London's Great Fire had destroyed much of the city. Dr. Nicholas Barbones (called "Barebones" by his contemporaries) was a speculative builder who gambled on his vision of neighborhoods filled with uniform tenements and block-like houses. He cleverly persuaded unwary investors to give him money time and again; gathered the workers, wood, stone, and tools he needed; and often realized fortunes by cramming the lower classes into his tract housing. After one success, he would go after another fortune; soon he had become the creator of many London neighborhoods. But in the end his gambling led him too far and he died penniless.

The derby-hatted contractor is no doubt seeing that the foreman and workers are building these Library of Congress cabinets to specifications. (National Archives)

Most of his successors in the Victorian Age played for smaller stakes; a typical builder might complete fewer than six houses in a year. A few made fortunes completing the railways and docks that civil engineers had designed, or else constructing neighborhoods of homes in the growing cities. Thomas Cubitt is said to have paid for and built much of London's Pimlico and Belgravia districts. He kept more than one thousand workers on hand, and his Pimlico workshops covered 11 acres. He began the builder's practice of employing workmen to do everything from masonry to plastering, rather than allowing the client to contract such artisans as needed. Thus, the job of building contractor—the person who made a living by supplying everything needed to see a building to completion—had appeared.

With all this building, the designers could count on a good deal of money and a high place in their society. An architect's office would most often set its fee at 5 percent of a project's cost. Great sums could be made by the successful. Sir Gilbert Scott left an estate of 130,000 pounds, or about $650,000. Sir Robert Smith would take no job that did not pay him 10,000 pounds; among his designs are the British Museum and King's College.

In 19th-century England the work of the architect became very defined, narrowed down to design. The contractor and the speculative builder now played their own well-defined roles in building projects too. The architect made designs of quality for people of quality. The profession bred its own family of journals, which reported on developments in theory and methods. Not everyone agreed on the importance of the work, however. One architect, dissatisfied with the work his profession was doing, described architecture as "a light, genteel employment, giving the position, social and financial, due to gentlemen and scholars." It is true that of the designs of the day, so many of which were lavishly rewarded, very few were good. In England and North America, architecture had stayed a profession with the most loosely woven rules. Qualifying as an architect was still too easy for too many; the profession often attracted men who were not seriously interested in or talented at building. Engineers often saw architecture not as building, but as something added to building. After a building had been raised, a little architectural design could be inflicted on it, they seemed to believe. The architects generally agreed. Sir Gilbert Scott, who had made the greatest success of architecture in his generation, declared its purpose to be "to decorate construction." John Ruskin, a great dissident art critic of the age, said much the same thing: "Ornamentation is the principal part of architecture." The new rich had a taste for degraded Gothic architecture, and architects were glad to oblige them by sticking gables and peaks onto their work wherever the patrons liked. They made the fulfillment of whims their business. The trade focused heavily on *revivals*, imitation after imitation of past styles.

The training of an engineer was rigorous; he could not do his work without understanding a strict and complicated system of science. The critic Joseph Gwilt, looking on architects in 1827, wrote that "Mathematics have, perhaps, been too much neglected....The consequence has been the establishment of a new branch of art whose professors [practitioners] are called civil Engineers."

Order had left architecture for a new profession. Who was an architect and who was not had become clearer, but what an architect should know and how it should be taught were still vague. Most learned their work as apprentices in an established architect's office. What an apprentice learned depended on the master architect's interest and the apprentice's own resourcefulness. Apprenticeship lasted anywhere from two to five years. Boys selected as apprentices (14 was thought a good age to start training) might live with their masters while picking up the elements of theory. Some architects kept a dozen teenaged apprentices in the household at once. Afterwards, the boys traveled if they could, then joined an office. Some took evening classes at academies; but their

While workers are exposed to sun and rain, more formally dressed architects and contractors are generally better protected from the elements. (From Gems From Judge, *1922)*

most important lessons were whatever they could teach themselves sketching in their free time.

The profession was just as muddled in the United States during the 1800's. There, just a century before, any sort of designer in building had been a novelty. A few had excelled, but most master carpenters had followed books from England. James Gibbs's *Book of Architecture* provided printed plans in the Georgian manner, from which the carpenters might work directly. The English founded their Royal Institute of Architects in 1837, to set some standards for their profession's output. An architectural hopeful could not hope to find academic training in the United States, however, until the Massachusetts Institute of Technology founded its graduate school of architecture in 1867.

With that, at least, a movement had begun. Through the next decades one after another of America's old universities began teaching the fundamentals of the profession. American architects took their model from France. The *Ecole des Beaux Arts*, founded in 1671, had converted architecture into an orderly series of rules, which could be understood by anyone with the desire and intelligence necessary to master them. American architects could and did set the same standards for themselves, finding some agreement about what their work was and how well it was being practiced. The Ecole des Beaux Arts divided its students into two levels; one advanced from the lower to the higher as the experts judged project after project and awarded points for how close the work came to the way fine architecture was supposed to be. Graduation was proof that one was an architect. All American architecture students with the money—and the profession attracted many gentlemen—traveled to France and the "Beaux-Arts." An Institute of Design opened in New York City, offering night classes taught by Paris-trained American architects. The Massachusetts Institute of Technology and Cornell University also hired French design professors. State governments set standards of their own. Illinois had been the first to require a license for architectural practice, in 1897. This was the method that all the others seized upon. No one could build for a state's citizens unless a commission of architects approved by his state government had passed judgment on his training and honesty. Prospective architects had to pass written tests and then an oral examination. The state boards eventually agreed on minimum standards that would cover the country.

In England, the Royal Institute of British Architects (RIBA) set compulsory examinations for architectural candidates in 1882. Architecture entered the university curriculum, but the Institute claimed the right of approval over any such instruction; graduation from an approved program was equivalent to passing the Royal Institute's test. RIBA counted 6,000 full members in the 1920's; it did not gather all architects under its regulations, but its members set the profession's standard. Across the ocean, the American Institute of Architecture performed a similar function. In 1960 it included almost half of all American architects on its rolls—a majority of those architects actually practicing. The Institute members abide by "Standards of Professional Practice" that forbid competitive bidding and executing a design before a commission is awarded. In 1980, 79,500 architects were at work in the United States. Architects work as salaried employees of building and real estate companies, or in architecture partnerships. The latter is the route to the profession's highest pay and greatest prestige.

The universities and professional institutes educate architects today—among them a small but increasing number of women. It is still possible to begin as an

Modern architects do much of their work at the drawing board. (From Men: A Pictorial Archive From Nineteenth-Century Sources, *by Jim Harter, Dover, 1980)*

apprentice, but the training is long; in the United States, most states require 12 years of such apprenticeship. At a university or professional institute, the American architect is taught physics, advanced mathematics, structural engineering, familiarity with materials, and the history of the profession, as well as topics in the newly important area known as *environmental controls*—the mechanical systems needed to keep building properly lit, warmed, and ventilated.

Civil engineers begin their studies with undergraduate courses at college. After graduation, the candidate works under supervision for several years, in a kind of apprenticeship. In many countries, such as Great Britain and the United States, this ends when the engineer can pass a set examination.

Architecture has bred a more specialized profession, that of the *restorer*. For thousands of years, whatever people built, they eventually allowed to fall down. If the stone or wood was needed, they would pull down what had once been put up. A 17th-century pope ordered his favorite architect to refit the Roman Colosseum as a wool factory.

In later centuries, however, some architects took up commissions to restore great and aging edifices. Throughout the 19th century, they did their work relying on whim and notions that they took for artistic intuition. In the process, many fine old castles and churches were savaged. Martin Brill, a British architect and historian of his trade, sharply criticized James Wyatt, a president of the Royal Academy as well as a successful architect and restorer, "whose surgical treatment of our cathedrals earned him the nickname of 'The Destroyer.'"

Restorers now practice a science sometimes more rigorous than architecture. Some are architects, refurbishing handsome old houses for their clients. But restoration specialists aim at nothing less than undoing time's damage; they clean off disfigurements, and prevent decay and collapse. Buildings that have already buckled are essentially rebuilt. Technically, these two jobs are known as restoration and *reconstruction*, but both are supervised by the restorer. No one can be absolutely sure what an old building originally looked like, but teams of scientists—*physicists*, *chemists*, *archaeologists*, and *engineers*—aid the restorer in trying to visualize the building as it once was. The architect trained in restoration then goes to work on the building's shell, trying not so much to re-create its original appearance as to save what is left without transforming the building into something it never was. Most nations have government programs of monument preservation, designed to save their store of cultural wealth. The United Nations Educational, Scientific and Cultural Organization operates an international program for the same purpose.

Working closely with architects and contractors for thousands of years have been *surveyors*, who measure distances, elevations, and angles of orientation of sites all over the Earth. They help architects and contractors decide how a building should be situated on the ground. By 2700 B.C. they were already at work, for the Great Pyramid at Ghiza, built at that time, is precisely square and oriented to the points of the compass—evidence of the craft of these early surveyors.

These specialists also use their skills to help determine with great accuracy the boundary lines between properties. Surveying to mark property boundary lines has been carried on since at least 1400 B.C., in both Mesopotamia and Egypt; boundary markers have been found from this period, as well as one depiction of two men apparently dividing a field using knotted cords.

Using techniques from mathematics (surveying has both gained from and given much to geometry and trigonometry), astronomy, engineering, and nautical navigation, among other fields, surveyors developed a wide range of instruments, starting with the early plumb bobs and levels. The modern Scientific Revolution provided other instruments that could be turned to surveying uses. Lasers have been used since the 1960's to measure distances as well as to check alignments.

While many surveyors have worked "in the small" with architects and contractors, others have taken a wider view and have worked with *mapmakers* or *cartographers*. Aerial photographs and, more recently, satellite pictures have allowed surveyors to prepare increasingly accurate large-scale surveys, especially with the aid of computers to process data.

Surveyors generally work in teams, with assistants called *rod workers* or *chain workers* physically handling many of the measuring devices. Surveyors do not generally require college degrees for their work, but combine on-the-job experience with two to three years of technical training, preparatory to passing a licensing examination. As a result, the pay is not high, even for experienced surveyors heading a small team. Certain kinds of surveying, such as surveying for petroleum companies, may be more lucrative, however.

For related occupations in this volume, *Builders*, see the following:

Carpenters
Construction Laborers
Masons
Plasterers and Other Finishing Workers
Plumbers
Roadbuilders
Shipwrights

For related occupations in other volumes of the series, see the following:

in *Artists and Artisans* (to be published Fall 1986):

Glassblowers
Jewelers
Painters
Potters
Sculptors

in *Communicators* (to be published Fall 1986):

Scribes

in *Financiers and Traders*:
   Stewards and Supervisors
in *Harvesters* (to be published Spring 1987):
   Farmers, Gardeners
in *Healers* (to be published Spring 1987):
   Physicians and Surgeons
in *Leaders and Lawyers*:
   Political Leaders
in *Manufacturers and Miners* (to be published Fall 1987):
   Miners and Quarriers
in *Scholars and Priests* (to be published Fall 1987):
   Monks and Nuns, Priests, Scholars, Teachers
in *Scientists and Technologists* (to be published Spring 1988):
   Cartographers
   Chemists
   Engineers
   Mathematicians
   Physicists
   Scientific Instrument Makers

Carpenters

Carpenters make things out of wood, a material that is common in most parts of the world. Throughout history, wood has been used for a wide variety of items, from bowls and spoons to houses. Until the last 400 years, most carpenters did not specialize. A given carpenter was likely to build tables as well as homes. Then, some carpenters began to specialize in fine work and became *furniture-makers*. Others continued their general work and became known as *rough carpenters*. It is these rough carpenters we focus on here.

Wood does not need to be quarried; it comes growing out of the ground, and, though strong enough for building, can be knocked to earth, stripped ready for use, and shaped by the simplest tools. Living in uncut forests, ancient peoples turned to the wood around them for the materials with which to build their homes. People built their own houses, using tools that probably did not go beyond a simple knife and an axehead lashed to a branch. Several thousand years before Jesus Christ—himself a carpenter—the people of Britain made their houses with wooden walls, floors, and roofs; split-off tree trunks set in a row through the interior supported the ceiling. In other regions, including both Scandinavia and the Himalayas, people built themselves log cabins, much like those of the North American pioneers.

In the ancient world's more advanced countries, wood was used in more sophisticated ways. Knowing how to work properly with wood came to be a skill, and the carpenter's trade emerged. Early carpenters used a variety of tools, starting with the *axe*. Egyptian carpenters of 1500 B.C. used *chisels* to split the wood and cut joints so that separate pieces could be fitted together; the *awl*, a very slender sort of spike, was used to bore holes; the wood's surface was cut smooth with an *adze*, forerunner of the *plane*. Early carpenters also had special tools for measuring, cutting, and finishing wood. For the past 3,500 years this set of tools has stayed roughly the same, with only minor changes and additions appearing in one country or another.

Carpenters used their tools to split and cut away at the wood, reducing it to planks and beams ready for use. In Egypt, a desert country with just a scattering of trees, wood was often imported from Lebanon. The wooden planks produced by carpenters were very expensive and used primarily for display; few people could afford enough planks to make a floor or wall. Instead, a noble might use wood panels to cover a conspicuous wall. Using even that much wood was quite an impressive way of displaying wealth. On moving, a noble did not leave stone or wood with the house; they were pulled up and packed away, carried to the new site in caskets, and delivered to the builder for use only under supervision.

In Egypt, carpenters used wood primarily for decoration. In other countries, however, planks and beams were available in sufficient numbers to play a useful part in lifting up a house. Greek and Roman homes had walls of brick and stone, floors and roof rafters of wood; on top of a stone foundation rested the timber frame of the house, the structure within which everything was fitted. Until this century, building such frames was the mainstay of the building carpenter's profession.

Egyptian carpenters were owned by the nobles who employed them, and the fate of carpenters in other ancient nations was not much better. Sometimes carpenters were slaves; generally they were among a country's many low-paid workers. Most were forgotten after death, though in Carthage, a powerful North African trading city, carpenters were honored for the work they did in building the nation's great merchant fleet, the finest of the Mediterranean.

Carpenters held a very different position in ancient India. In the last centuries before the Christian era, carpenters were respected, but not so much for their skill as for their place in the scheme of things. India's priests had looked upon the world and, in trying to understand everything that they saw, developed a vision of the universe as a great tree, characterized by strength, many branches, and unending growth. This image worked its way into custom and sacred usages. Because a new building was made of wood, it had to be sanctified by priests. Carpenters, since they worked with the wood of the great tree's representatives, were placed in an eminent position above India's other workers. The carpenter personally selected the trees to be used for building a new house, and—along with the *priest* and *astrologers*—blessed and made ready a recently raised house for its newly wed couple. In theory, a house could not be built unless such a couple had commissioned it and a priest was involved in the process. However, carpenters often built houses without priestly involvement and carried on a retail trade for whatever customers came along.

Carpenters built in nations all over the world. Wherever there were trees, whether in China or Central

America's Mayan Empire, people employed specialists to build with wood. Wood was the favorite building material in China, except for walls and other large public structures. In his *Science and Civilization in China*, Joseph Needham put it quite simply: "No Chinese house could be a proper dwelling for the living, or a proper place of worship for the gods, unless it were built in wood and roofed in tile." Unfortunately, carpenters—being manual or mechanical laborers—were ignored by the great record-keeping scholars of China. Therefore, we know almost nothing about their lives, and what little we know about their work has survived mostly by accident. Master-carpenters, especially those working in imperial workshops, often drafted manuals of procedure, such as the *Mu Ching* (Timberwork Manual). These included elaborate sets of rules for construction, depending on the type of building. From the manuals we learn that proportion was extremely important to Chinese builders. The crossbeams, the rafters, and the incline of the steps or

ramps were all carefully related to one another. Eleventh-century scholar Shen Kua, for example, noted that:

> ...of ramps (and steps) there are three kinds, steep, easy-going and intermediate. In palaces these gradients are based upon a unit derived from the imperial litters. Steep ramps are ramps for ascending which the leading and trailing bearers have to extend their arms fully down and up respectively...Easy-going ramps are those for which the leaders use elbow length and the trailers shoulder height...intermediate ones are negotiated by the leaders with downstretched arms and trailers at shoulder height...

In China, there was a sharp social distinction between working carpenters—even master-carpenters who wrote construction manuals and produced the finest buildings for the emperor—and *architects* who designed the buildings and were "white-collar" scholars working in the government.

In medieval Japan, a land largely bare of metal or building stone, giant carpenters' guilds did the country's building, and employed many other workers to help them.

Carpenters often worked in teams, cutting the wood on site and hauling it up to form the frames. (From Picture Book of Graphic Arts, 1500–1800)

Carpenters no longer did all the work with their own hands. *Forest workers* felled the trees and broke them apart; they split the trunks with wedges and mallets, then turned the wood into planks with their adzes and axes. The planks were then floated down Japan's rivers on barges to the towns, where carpenters joined the boards and beams into houses. In a small village, a single carpenter might build a house alone. But city carpenters, who raised temples and great homes, worked in teams; a *foreman* acted as mastermind on a project's site, making all measurements personally and supervising the workers with their materials. One carpenter cut beams to shape; another made floorboards; a third made braces for the roof. Then, having cut out the pieces, the team raised them all in place. Although Japan is a small country with a population that increased only slowly, the storms and earthquakes that struck the islands from out of the Pacific meant constant rebuilding—and work for carpenters.

Carpentry fared differently in medieval Europe. There ignorance, isolation, and poverty followed the fall of the Roman Empire in the fifth century A.D. Carpentry skills did survive, however, and even flourished in some areas. The carpenters of the German overlords had a surprising degree of skill. For one thing, they used an early version of the *lathe*: the carpenter held a piece of wood against a rapidly turning blade, which quickly rounded it into shape. Compared to models that would come many years later, the German instrument was fairly limited, but it still allowed for versatile work.

But most people in Europe did not live like Germany's tribal kings. A peasant's house was made of mud and sticks. In England during the Dark Ages, from the fifth to the ninth century, the old Roman civilization died quickly and left very little behind. Carpentry returned to its ancient forest days. Warlords lived in what they called *halls*. These were rough-timbered buildings that were like oversized barns. Farm animals and the local "nobility" lived together, the animals in lofts overhead. In later centuries, aristocrats descended from these warlords would proudly call their own mansions *halls*. The original barn-like style of the hall was followed for a long time, growing richer, larger, and more elaborate, until by the 18th century, its origins were no longer distinguishable.

During this period, teams of carpenters were employed by the Roman Catholic church to build churches of wood. A *master of works*, usually a priest, oversaw the building. Carpenters worked as much in the forest as on the project site. The master sent them to cut down trees and cart them back. These carpenters were considered mere workmen rather than craftsmen. The large team of carpenters who built the ninth-century church of St. Aubin were all ordered whipped when they returned with timber of the wrong measurements.

Carpenters of the early Middle Ages had an uncertain existence. After completing their work, they were left by their employers to find a new project or starve. But in later centuries, as skills advanced and projects grew more ambitious, carpenters came to be treated more as skilled

Carpenters used a wide variety of tools to prepare wood for the houses, mills, bridges, ships, and other structures that they built. (By Jost Amman, from The Book of Trades, *late 16th century)*

artisans than as disposable sources of brute labor. Carpenters, in fact, came to stand very high among craft workers. Once again they were building houses, this time with walls as well as frames of timber. Carpenters often acted as patrons to *plasterers*, *thatchers*, and *tilers*, who finished the homes that the carpenters had begun.

By the 11th to the 14th centuries, Europe's builders had begun great cathedrals and palaces of stone. Once the people of the Middle Ages had learned again how to build with stone, the most powerful would accept nothing else. Carpenters were employed to build the scaffolds and pilings that helped the stone builders, called *masons*, in their work. In addition, just as the *master-mason* would design one of these great buildings, so the master-carpenter would design its roof; Master Hugh Erland, for example, is credited with building the roof of England's Westminster Hall. Such a roof could be the size of a playing field; designing its structure took considerable thought. The master led a team of his best men in their workshop, laboring slowly together. Oxen and carts drew the pieces to the work site. The carpenters did not worry much about finding wood that was seasoned (dried out) enough to use in building. Jobs generally lasted so long that whatever wood they chose would be seasoned enough by the time the carpenters were ready to use it.

Carpenters of that time did not wear uniform clothing. For many centuries, drawings show them dressed in simple belted tunics, the tunics sometimes knotted up about the waist so as not to catch on tools. We know about the tools of that period from a poem called *The Debate of the Carpenter's Tools*. The poem is a whimsical fantasy in which the tools argue about which is the most useful. The list is very long: three kinds of axes; two chisels; an adze; a whetstone for sharpening the other tools; a "pricking knife," or kind of pencil; a plane; a rule; a crowbar; a sort of awl called the "draught-nayle;" and many different measuring devices.

The long list of tools gives some indication of how much skill carpenters of the late Middle Ages had to bring to their work. Wood could be made into so many different things and worked in so many different ways that the demand for a certain wooden product might—and often did—support a specialized carpenter. Through experimentation carpenters expanded their skills, and many of these skills became separate crafts. Some carpenters did the humble work. Enough money was spent on carpenters and wood to support men who simply planed boards or built scaffolds for their livings. Others in the new trades made specialties out of woodwork that was far more advanced. In the last centuries of the Middle Ages, for example, *turners* began to shape wood on lathes as their craft. From round cross-sections of wood they fashioned the component pieces of furniture.

Like other artisans of the late Middle Ages, carpenters formed guilds, standardizing trade rules and formalizing arrangements for training apprentices. Originally the guilds were not exclusively male in their membership, although they would later become so. Numerous guild records speak of "Brothers and Sisters" of the Carpenters' Company. But most women seem to have entered the trade only on the death of their husbands, whose place they were allowed to take at the guild and whose apprentices they could keep, if they chose to continue the business. That women were generally allowed into the trade only in the absence of their husbands is indicated by the 1554 ruling of the Worshipful Company of Carpenters:

> ...yt was agreyd be the Master & wardyns and the moste parte of the assestens that no woman shall come to the waters to by tymber bourde lath qtrs ponchons gystes & Raffters ther husbandes beyng in the town uppon payne to forfyt at evry tyme so fownd.

In Paris a new breed called *joiners* abandoned the carpenters for a guild of their own in 1371. They worked by a method called *paneling*, the fitting together of planed pieces of wood. Paneling was a great advance for carpentry: the joiners could turn out the first fine and light carpentry work to be seen in Europe since Roman times. Joiners became the most prosperous of the carpentry trade, patronized by the wealthiest clients. Other carpenters built the frames and walls of a house, but joiners made the interior, the surroundings within which the owners would live.

Using paneling, the joiners could fit out a room with amenities that older techniques were not delicate enough to match. They made wood panels, slender sills, and door frames. Before then, even rooms in fine houses had been simple boxes within walls, with a door and perhaps a gouged window showing the way out. The joiners' trade arose at the same time that Europeans were rediscovering how a dwelling could be transformed to suit their tastes and comfort. Joiners covered interior walls with wood, erected compact staircases, made it possible to build more doorways and windows, and framed those with wood as well.

Most important, the joiners finished fitting out a house by giving it furniture. Building carpenters of an earlier

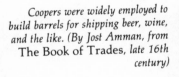

Coopers were widely employed to build barrels for shipping beer, wine, and the like. (By Jost Amman, from The Book of Trades, *late 16th century)*

time had also made some furniture, but it had been of rough quality, most often made with the lumber left over after a house frame had been built. Carpenters had never made much furniture, in any case; only a few of the nobility might own more than one or two pieces. This changed with the emergence of the specialist joiners. If there was enough wood for window sills, there was enough wood for more than one stool in a room. The furniture made by the joiners could be considered a part of the building, since it completed the house built for clients. Then again, the staircases, doorways, and window sills built by joiners could actually be considered furnishings: they did nothing to support the structure of the house; they were meant only to make the rooms within more convenient places to live. Joiners, working with building carpenters, had a job and a place in society much more like those of the *cabinetmakers*, who would soon form their own specialty of making furniture.

By the 16th century, as the Middle Ages drew to a close, more Europeans had the money to buy homes than ever before. Carpenters competed with masons, especially *bricklayers*, for the trade. Carpenters remained respected artisans, and they began to command more wealth and position than they had in the two centuries past. By the 17th century, carpenters in large cities became business people of substance, running storefront workshops or contracting teams for building projects. Masters of the carpentry guilds often acquired reputations for dressing very fashionably.

The craft of carpentry traveled westward when French and English settlers came to the New World during the 17th century. Professional carpenters traveled to Canada a few decades after the French had first settled along the St. Lawrence Valley. Being poor, England's colonies had little work for carpenters at first, since early colonists built their own homes. But an accessory craft developed to supply suitable building materials; colonists brought their wood to *sawyers*, who made their living by sawing planks.

Most settlers in the New World mastered a simple sort of carpentry as part of their survival, and professional carpenters were rare. When Southern plantation owners of the 18th century decided to use the money they had made from their tobacco and cotton crops to build fashionable mansions like those of English lords, they imported skilled artisans. The wood, plaster, and stone needed for the job could be found in America; but the people who knew how to do fine work with these materials—from supervisor to joiner—came from England, drawn by high wages. The slaves lent to carpenters as laborers quickly picked up the ideas behind the craft, however, and practice brought some of them up to a professional level. One planter hired a team of carpenters to build stables, a house, a barn, and outhouses—then fired them halfway through when he learned his slaves could complete the job.

In the 1740's and '50's, the Colonies became considerably more affluent, and the population wanted new and better homes. New England meetinghouses were both conceived and built by the village carpenters. Philadelphia, the Colonies' leading city, contained 1,500 homes in 1743; by 1760, the number had jumped to 2,969. Most of the new houses built surrounding the old city were made of timber. As Pennsylvania's towns spread and her forests were cut down, one man wrote to a friend in 1763: "What our people will do for fencing and firewood fifty years hence, I can't imagine."

The position and pay of the *master-builders* rose with their customers, and carpenters led the building trades. America did not have medieval-style guilds, but in the late 18th century Philadelphia's carpenters formed the country's first craft society, the Carpenter's Company of the City and County of Philadelphia. They did not consider themselves artisans, but rather proud professionals like physicians or lawyers. In Pennsylvania they could reach great social heights. Philadelphia had been founded by the Quakers, a sect that respected working with the hands as part of the life God had laid out for humankind.

There, the old gentry were ready to accept successful carpenters into their own numbers. The hall of the Carpenter's Company, built from 1768 to 1774, was on the scale of a major public building.

Some of the carpenters who mixed so comfortably with the established rich were actually working as *architects*, a profession not yet performed by one group of specialists. The great mansions of the day depended on the design of the wooden frames that supported them. *Master-carpenters* could find themselves taking on challenging intellectual work when they designed and supervised the building of such structures. Those who worked on the great projects were accomplished men, suited to move among professionals.

Carpenters did not stay architects for long, but while they did, the job was very important to their craft. Carpenters called *housewrights* designed and built houses. Other carpenters designed public buildings. The master-carpenter Robert Smith designed Nassau Hall and New College in Philadelphia, as well as serving as head carpenter for St. Paul's Cathedral. Samuel Powel, nicknamed the "rich carpenter," made his fortune by designing and building streets full of houses for small artisans and shopkeepers; he left a legacy of 90 houses, all filled with rent-paying families. These master-carpenters ran their profession, employing many workers below them. After the master-builders had given way to architects in the 19th century, all that remained to carpentry was manual labor. Carpenters as a craft then belonged to the working class.

An English manual called *The Book of Trades* gives us some details about carpenters and their work in 1804. The author remarks that carpenters are most often "those who do the rough work in the building of houses." Joiners do "the lighter kind of work" on the inside. But "most of those...brought up to the trade are both carpenters and joiners." (Furniture-making had become a separate specialty.) Carpentry workers had to buy their own set of tools; this cost "no less than ten and possibly more than

This 19th century English cooper is wearing traditional garb, including apron, breeches, and brewer's cap. (Authors' archives)

twenty pounds"—that is, from 125 to over 250 of today's dollars, a very large sum for an artisan of the time. The master-carpenter of a team issued tools, on loan, for such specialized decorative work as carved moldings.

The Book of Trades also tells about some of the humbler wood crafts, lesser offshoots of carpentry that shared the same materials and similar tools. *Coopers* made "casks, tubs,...pails, and sundry other items useful in domestic concerns," barrels being the most notable among them. Coopers split oak into strips called *staves*, then fastened these into a container; when bent, the staves fashioned a curving wall that continued in a full circle. The whole was secured with pegs and enclosing hoops, of wood or iron. The people of those days did not have much to store or hold; once the cooper had supplied the houses of an area with the barrels they needed, he had to move on, traveling to find work. Coopers carried a stock of hoops and staves, along with a hammer, an adze, rivets, and pegs. Much of their work came from odd repairs. In the more remote villages the cooper was the closest thing to a full-fledged carpenter.

Sawyers were still at work, earning as much as carpenters. Their work took a great deal of strength. The wood to be sawed was placed on two rods that supported it as it passed lengthwise above a trench. The trench ended in a pit where the sawyer's assistant, the *pitman*, stood. Standing on the ground above and straddling the wood, the sawyer guided a long *sash* or *pit saw*, which had handles on either end, down to the pitman. The two then worked it vertically, the pitman holding onto the saw's handles below to keep it steady. Leverage, the whole point of the situation, allowed the two men to cut apart vast amounts of timber, but the work took all their strength. This trade would not last for much longer; *The Book of Trades* remarks upon the appearance of *sawmills*, factories where machines powered by the flow of nearby rivers could do the work much faster than sawyers could.

While other artisans around them were absorbed into or replaced by factories in the 19th century, carpenters were not. They remained independent artisans—in Britain being distinguished by wearing a paper cap (later adopted by many other artisans) and breeches (replaced by trousers only late in the century). But machines now set the pace of society's work, and unorganized carpenters, by far the majority, were pressed harder and harder as their employers tried to make them keep up.

At the beginning of the machine age, during the Napoleonic Wars, many of London's carpenters already belonged to mutual aid societies; dues were collected into funds to be drawn on when a member was ill or out of work. A *glazier* (window installer) sent from the countryside to borrow money for his comrades complained that the carpenters who received him exchanged "significant glances" on hearing that his trade had no society for mutual aid. When unionization first gathered strength in the middle of the 19th century, the carpenters belonged to the largest and most militant union in both England and France.

By the 1860's and '70's, carpenters were being driven hard by their employers. Workshops, larger than any before, were presided over by a foreman who sat on a stool 10 feet above the workers' heads and gazed out over rows of benches. The workshops were run by simple rules: no one could look up and no one's hands could stop working. A carpenter told one London journalist: "A man working at such places is almost always in fear." Workshops turned out ornaments and house parts for the suburbs that were being built throughout most of the 19th century. The houses were being built in greater numbers than ever before and at greater speed. The contractors practiced what their carpenters called *scamping*: purposely demanding bad work because it could be done faster and cheaper. After having worked hard to acquire skills, carpenters were forced to abandon those skills, a source of much complaint with them. All the time, their wages were being lowered along with the level of skill demanded of them. Carpenters were not alone in their plight. Reformers and statisticians, investigating the London lower classes of the 1890's, found that carpenters lived relatively well in that only a third were in poverty.

Real change came, as it came for all working trades, in the 20th century. Unionization and social reform have removed carpenters a comfortable distance from poverty. At the same time, however, much of the carpenters' work has been handed over to machines, just where some employers always thought it belonged. Many houses today are assembled from components prepared in factories, where electrical tools operate with a power that goes far beyond human energy. Such machine tools, guided by workers, include the circular bench saw, the band saw, the planer, the mortiser (for cutting mortise joints), the molder, the sander, and others. As more and more of the components of a house are prepared in factories, there is less work to do on the building site itself. Building carpenters find a large part of their jobs taken out of their hands, and they are left to put in the proper order what others have already made.

Carpenters still prepare partitions for rooms and build the roofs of smaller buildings. Independent carpenters live in many suburbs and towns, employing a few helpers, and doing work of this sort: repairs, installing doors, and making additions to existing houses. Carpenters also work on large construction projects, sinking foundation beams called *piles* and erecting temporary work platforms called *scaffolds*. Some work as *timberers*, constructing frames to support the sides of excavated pits for excavators or demolition engineers—as some of their calling have done in mines for many centuries. One sort of work that calls for a whole new order of special skills is that of building *forms*, large wooden molds into which concrete is poured, then allowed to set. Forms are used to shape the components of buildings made from concrete.

An apprentice carpenter in the United States must be between 17 and 27 years of age. The candidate applies to a board consisting of representatives of both the employers and the unions. Much of the four-year training is on the job, but an apprentice also attends school, a departure from earlier times. A high school diploma is a requirement for entry; apprentices are taught all aspects of the craft, including mathematics and the reading of

Until the rise of machine-driven mills, sawing was generally done with one person above and the other below, often in a pit. (From Diderot's Encyclopedia, *late 18th century*)

Coopers became increasingly important, more often working in large-scale establishments as industrialization spread. (From Diderot's Encyclopedia, *late 18th century)*

blueprints. On graduation, the apprentice must pass a written exam and submit a finished building project for approval, much like the *master piece* required of apprentices by Europe's old guilds. Carpentry work has been an all-male occupation for most of its history, but some women are now entering the field under equal opportunity regulations. Wages are settled by negotiations between the carpentry unions and the employers, who are, for the most part, building contractor firms. Carpenters on building sites cannot work all through the year, but even so their earnings place them ahead of many other workers. The trade is still flourishing, with 830,000 carpenters working in the United States in 1970, roughly one-third of all construction workers.

For related occupations in this volume, *Builders*, see the following:
    Architects and Contractors
    Masons
    Plasterers and Other Finishing Workers
    Shipwrights

For related occupations in other volumes of the series, see the following:

in *Artists and Artisans* (to be published Fall 1986):
  Furniture-Makers

in *Harvesters* (to be published Spring 1987):
  Farmers

in *Manufacturers and Miners* (to be published Fall 1987):
  Miners and Quarriers

  in *Scholars and Priests* (to be published Fall 1987):
Priests

in *Scientists and Technologists* (to be published Spring 1988):
  Astrologers

Construction Laborers

To raise a building takes money, planning, and the exercise of a dozen different kinds of crafts. But it also requires sheer physical effort. Strength makes a building possible. For thousands of years, this strength could come only from human beings—*construction laborers*. Whatever did not take training, the laborer would do. Throughout history, laborers have not only performed simple, routine tasks but also supplied a truly awesome amount of muscle. Only in the past century and a half have people found ways to replace this muscle with the machine.

Early architects had to assemble the equivalent building strength of our cranes and tractors. Their main unit of power was the human being, so armies of laborers—willing or unwilling—became important con-

59

tributors to history. Egypt's thousands of pyramid-builders were among the first; they have become something of a legend today. The Great Pyramid of the pharaoh Cheops was built by piling 2,300,000 stone blocks. Each block had an average weight of two and a half tons. The equipment for moving the blocks was quite simple—ropes for pulling, sledges and ramps as surfaces for the blocks to be pulled over. What mattered most were the men who did the pulling. Traditionally, people have spoken of the "slave armies" who built the pyramids. But in truth most of the workers were hired and paid salaries. The fact that they were paid kept them from being slaves. Of course, that does not mean their lives were easy. The builders in charge did not always feel it necessary to pay punctually, and when money or food ran short, the workers sometimes starved.

Egyptian laborers were organized as an army: they lived in barracks with each man assigned to work with a

For thousands of years, most construction laborers were manual workers, like these working on the Suez Canal. (From Egypt, by Clara Erskine Clement, 1903)

group under an unquestioned leader and disciplinarian. Laboring on the pharaoh's monument was like modern army duty in other ways as well: a man was called up for a set number of years and served his time. Some Egyptian men volunteered for part-time services. Most of the people in Egypt were peasants. The Nile flooded its banks each year, watering the fields; after it did so, the *farmer* had to look for other work until the harvest. Some farmers apparently volunteered for work on the pyramids, being let off each season in time to look after their crops.

Unlike the ancient Egyptians, the Romans of the first century A.D. more often assembled their construction laborers through force. For their massive construction projects, the state pulled together gangs of unskilled slaves, criminals, prisoners of war, and soldiers, especially in time of peace, when they were otherwise idle. When the construction was being done on the frontiers of the expanding empire, these laborers were often settled in the region, tending by their presence to bind the area more firmly to Rome.

At the same time, on the other side of the world, the Chinese followed similar procedures of obtaining and settling workers to build early versions of the Great Wall. Criminals, exiles, political dissidents, soldiers, and local farmers in the off-season all were pressed into service to build the massive barrier, made largely of stone in the northeast and tamped earth in the west. Since the wall was meant to defend China against marauding nomads from the Eurasian Steppe, the Chinese apparently started by building freestanding stone towers, in which workers and soldiers would be housed and protected. Then they began to build the wall itself out from the towers in both directions, finally forming a continuous line. Starting in the third century B.C. and expanding and rebuilding over the centuries, the Chinese eventually extended their Great Wall to almost 4,000 miles. Often, apparently, construction laborers were settled in the area in which they built, acting as part of the protective force and also tilling the land to feed the frontier workers.

In later centuries, the Incas of South America took a somewhat different approach to the problem of construction labor; they forced conquered peoples into service. As they created and unified their elongated empire, the Incas broke up potential opposition by massive resettlement policies. Tribes were moved around the empire at will, each being assigned a particular construction task, such as building a bridge, carving out a road, or constructing shelters for official travelers. These tribes were expected to carry out the construction and also to maintain it, for which they received a portion of the empire's grain supply. The system became so widely accepted in the culture that, even long after the Incas were out of power, many of these tribes continued to keep up the maintenance work that had been assigned to them.

The kings of medieval Europe had their castles built by laborers who had been forced into service. The castles were not monuments; they were protection, and the kings wanted them built quickly. Soldiers patrolled the countryside, dragging workers, skilled and unskilled, to the building site. A great lord could do the same, after he had paid the king for a license to do so.

The Catholic church, on the other hand, hired workmen to raise the great medieval cathedrals. Escaped serfs and the younger sons of large peasant families were glad to find work on a building project. They mixed mortar, quarried stone, cut timber and carried it from the forests, pushed stone and plaster in wheelbarrows. The laborers' job was to supply what strength was needed to make the skilled workers' jobs move more easily. Laborers carried everything the skilled workmen did not want to lift, and earned—on the average—less than half a *mason's* pay. The laborers who worked on the cathedrals were not organized into an army the way Egyptian laborers had been. The building of a cathedral was a slow process that was expected to take generations. A laborer might be worn down to an early death, but he would not be yoked with a hundred of his fellows to the same block of stone, as Egyptian laborers had been.

In medieval times, hand-operated cranes were used to haul loads of materials to workers above. (From Life of St. Alban, *12th century, Trinity College, Dublin)*

Cathedral laborers did have some hope. They were on the scene, watching skills being used. Some learned the skills, and became *builders* rather than laborers. A few worked their way to *master-builders*, the masterminds of work sites. But most laborers led very hard lives. Devotional stories tell of lords and ladies who bent their necks, dragging rock to finish one of the Church's cathedrals. Less well known is the story of a nobleman who wanted to atone for a murder he had committed: he went to work anonymously, refusing pay. The other workers resented him for working without pay; after a week, they gathered around the man and beat him to death. Volunteers did not last long in an age when not many jobs did more than keep their workers alive; laborers felt threatened by anyone who was willing to work without pay.

Most of a laborer's work, in any age, was lifting, digging, and pushing—moving all the material that had to be rearranged for a building to stand. People experimented over the centuries to make lifting, digging, and pushing, and thus building, easier. Wire rope has been found in the remains of the ancient city of Pompeii. The wire was used in a first-century A.D. crane powered by slaves running on a treadmill. The Roman writer Vitruvius described its workings in his *Architecture*. A similar crane reappears in England in 1174. It was used to lift stone blocks for the rebuilding of Canterbury Cathedral. By the 16th century, European canal-builders knew how to build locks and sluices that allowed them to use the power of the ocean to do part of their work. At high tide the water would be penned up inside a lock or sluice; at low tide, the water would be let loose and wash away tons of earth. This technique was still used at the start of the 20th century in digging parts of the Panama Canal.

Such primitive techniques and tools, however, had been experiments of limited use or methods of last resort. Until the Industrial Revolution, the strength of a laborer remained the main source of power for construction. Then in the 18th century, Europeans mastered steam power; digging machines powered by steam engines could do the work that before had fallen to the squadrons of laborers. In 1801 a steam engine drove the piles (foundation columns laid beneath the earth) of London's new dock. In 1837 W.S. Otis of the United States invented the single-cylinder vertical steam engine; a steam-powered shovel, suspended from a crane, was able to swivel in a half-circle. The English imported shipments of the *steam shovels* to build their railways in the 1840's. A steam shovel able to swivel in a full circle was introduced 40 years later. From Hungary, in the 1860's, came a vast pod able to mix concrete: steam power kept an encircling belt shaking the mixture without stopping. A steam-powered *road roller* followed, able to level out earth simply by being driven forward. The Americans developed the first one suitable for widespread commercial use in 1904; 30 years after that, they fixed a concave shovel to its front and invented the *bulldozer*. Builders in the United States discarded steam power for electric power in the 1890's: they took up gasoline in 1913, and the even more powerful diesel fuel in 1924. Each improvement added new force.

Today, these powerful building machines have been adopted all over the world, and have been elaborated in many different makes and models. A crane that revolves, for example, is called a *jib crane*. An *overhead traveler* crane does not revolve, but instead moves on its base at right angles. A jib crane can be fixed or else equipped with wheels. Most are powered by electricity, and can lift and move a ton in two and a half minutes. Not all machines have this many different variations, however; some are quite simple. The *bulldozer* stays much the same through any of its models. An *air compressor* does no more than suck air and then project it through tubing, forcing it with enough speed to power workers' automatic hand tools.

Once, the moving of great weights had been a monumental task that required the efforts of many men over a long period of time. Today, we casually take the new power of machines for granted. In the spring of 1981, the driver of a bulldozer demolished an 18th-century mansion in the English countryside in three hours. His firm had been hired to destroy the mansion's outhouses, but the driver misunderstood what was to be done. He arrived a day before the work was scheduled and didn't find out his mistake until it was too late.

A new group of workers—*operational engineers*, also called operative or operating engineers—has been trained to run these powerful machines. Operating the machinery is not always complicated. Driving a bulldozer means pushing buttons that send it forward or back, lift the shovel or lower it. The operator of a tower crane has to climb up a ladder to a control booth in the crane's mast. Working the machine takes self-confidence, as well as a good eye for the tricks of distance. But what makes an *operational engineer* out of a laborer is reliability. A good operational engineer is someone who can be trusted to work at many times human strength without causing destruction. With all the power at hand, the laborer cannot use it casually. The strength of their machines is the chief hazard to the operators themselves; they must put up with the noise and jolting that come with being locked inside a machine many times human size and power. Work is done in rain or snow only in emergency situations, for the operator cannot take the chance of the machine getting out of hand.

Most operational engineers begin as *truck drivers* or helpers around the work site. They take care of the machines, then are allowed, under guidance, to work the smaller ones for a few years. The International Union of Operative Engineers and the Associated General Contractors of America—that is, both the operators' union and their employers—favor a three-year apprenticeship program. On-the-job training is accompanied by over 140 hours of classroom instruction. Apprentices graduate with skills that are not complex, but that together qualify them to work all the basic construction machines. Such graduates are officially recognized as *universal equipment operators*.

In 1980, about 270,000 operative engineers were at work in the United States. Fewer than 10 percent—one of

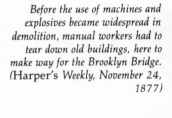

Before the use of machines and explosives became widespread in demolition, manual workers had to tear down old buildings, here to make way for the Brooklyn Bridge. (Harper's Weekly, November 24, 1877)

the smallest percentages for any sort of building worker—work for themselves. Usually only the construction companies have the money to buy and maintain the machines with which operative engineers make their living. They earn, on the average, $11 to $14 an hour; bad weather and building lulls, however, often prevent them from accumulating income steadily throughout the year. An apprentice starts with 70 percent of full hourly pay.

Changes in methods of construction bring out new specialties among construction laborers. Most large buildings of the 20th century have been raised with steel as their skeleton. Steel allows buildings to reach very great heights. The 1912 Woolworth Tower set a world record at 765 feet; today, Chicago's Sears Tower holds the record at almost twice that height: 1,450 feet.

The construction process is a highly mechanized one. After bulldozers and steam shovels open the earth, a

Doing very different construction from their forebears, these iron workers are raising steel on the 32nd floor of the Esso Building in New York City. (National Archives, Records of the United States Information Agency, 306-PS-54-186, 1954)

foundation is laid, and then cranes begin to lift in place, piece by piece, a superstructure of steel girders. The job cannot be completed totally by machine, however. The pieces have to be fitted firmly together and fastened securely by workers on the scene. From the vantage point of the heavy machine operators, what these people do seems to be a delicate adjustment. In fact, however, the job involves struggling with pieces of steel heavy enough to crush a person.

The specialists who do this job are called *ironworkers*. Ironworkers are laborers: they manage great weights or look after operations that are in themselves fairly simple. However, they do their work hundreds of feet above the ground, pacing along girders and scaffolding; there is an element of danger to their job that makes them an exclusive and well-paid type of laborer. They work on any great structure made from steel—dams, power plants, skyscrapers.

Many ironworkers have little formal education and therefore little hope of obtaining other high-paying work. Doing exhausting work is something they have been prepared for; doing it at dangerous heights is something they are ready for if the money is right. Irish immigrants to the United States in the 1860's were among the first to specialize in ironworking. Native Americans are the best known for taking up this work—so well known that many people assume that native Americans are born with a superior sense of balance. Various tribes from Canada and the northeastern United States joined the trade when building with iron first began in the late 19th century. According to one account, a bridge constructed over Canada's St. Lawrence River passed through the Caughnawoga reservation. To stay on the good side of the reservation's inhabitants, the builders opened up jobs to them. The members of the tribe proved to be outstanding ironworkers. When that project ended in 1886, many pulled up stakes and followed the high-paying jobs to big cities. By the next century high-steel construction was popularly thought of as a native American specialty.

Vertical girders are called *columns*. The horizontal girders that connect the columns are called *headers*. Smaller girders, called *beams*, run between headers. Cranes lift all of these for the first few floors, working from the ground. Then a smaller crane, the *derrick*, is lifted to the topmost level, where it is used to build the level above. As the building rises, the derrick is lifted from floor to floor. One group of ironworkers, called the *raising gang*, looks after the raising of the derrick. The raising gang is made up of six workers, plus a *pusher (foreman)*.

A large building may employ a hundred ironworkers working together at several different types of jobs to construct its skeleton. *Connectors*, working two to a team, take hold of the headers lifted by the derrick. When the derrick has brought a header to the right height, the connectors work it into the right position, fitting each end home against a column. This job takes more strength than any other job an ironworker can do; most connectors give it up when they pass 30. The *bolters-up* climb with buckets of bolts, securing the girders; a hundred bolts may be needed for one intersection. The *plumbing-up gang* has to adjust the columns, just as connectors adjust headers. They use turnbuckles and cables to cinch the columns, so that all are aligned and perfectly vertical. The *detail gang* manages the subsidiary girders that can be added in by hand.

As ironworkers finish off a floor, the other construction workers arrive—*glaziers*, *electricians*, *plumbers*, and many more. Five thousand people—still mostly white men, with few Blacks or women, despite equal opportunity programs—may work on one large building at the same time. The ironworkers stay separate, high above.

American ironworkers belong to the International Association of Bridge, Structural, and Ornamental Ironworkers. *Ornamental ironworking* is the installation of iron or steel additions to finished buildings, including fire escapes and stairways. *Reinforcing ironworking*, a third specialty, is the placing of iron bars in molds of concrete to reinforce the concrete; the concrete hardens with the iron as its center. *Structural ironworking*, the types described in detail in the preceding paragraphs, is practiced by most ironworkers. There were 116,000 structural ironworkers in America in 1980. Like the operative engineers, few ironworkers are self-employed. Some are apprenticed; some make their way into the trade as helpers, and others just show up when a contractor needs general laborers. Apprenticeship rules are much the same as those for the operative engineers. Bad weather and layoffs affect the ironworker's earnings, as they do the operative engineer's. When work lulls become severe, some ironworkers become *boomers*, who travel out of the jurisdiction of their local union chapter, looking for a job. Some boomers take off because they want a change of scene. Older men, or those with families to support, become boomers only because they need work and there is none at home.

In global terms, these heavy equipment operators are rather an elite group. In many parts of the world, where population is large and growing and where industrialization is still at its early stages, construction laborers remain manual workers, doing by hand most of the heavy work involved in building. Even in India, which is sufficiently advanced technologically to have an operating nuclear energy plant, construction projects are often characterized by lines of people passing from one to the other buckets of earth dug out of the ground by construction laborers working with picks and shovels.

For related occupations in this volume, *Builders*, see the following:
    Architects and Contractors
    Masons
    Plasterers and Other Finishing Workers
    Plumbers
    Roadbuilders

For related occupations in other volumes of the series, see the following:

in *Helpers and Aides* (to be published Spring 1987):
   Drivers

in *Harvesters* (to be published Spring 1987):
Farmers

In *Warriors and Adventurers* (to be published Spring 1988):
   Robbers and Other Criminals
   Soldiers

Masons

Masons build with stone, brick, cement, and concrete. Their work began almost with building itself, in the Near East as early as 10,000 years ago. Buildings made completely of stone have been found in Mesopotamia dating to at least 3,000 years B.C. Egyptian records mention even earlier unnamed, and now lost, stone-built palaces and temples.

During this period, masons laboring in vast teams raised the Egyptian pyramids, legendary for their size and probably the best-known buildings in the world. Standing thousands of feet high outside Memphis, the early Egyptian capital, each one was a tomb for one of the pharaohs.

The workers, along with the many million tons of stone that they built with, were assembled at the pharaoh's command. The pharaoh, the priests, and the nobles held

73

the masons essentially as slaves. Although many of the construction laborers were free paid workers, these masons—like other skilled artisans—were tied to their masters. Masons belonged to guilds of a sort, but these are likely to have been intended as a way for their masters to control and keep track of them: the only rule that has survived the centuries is that once born into the craft, a mason could try no other work. When the pharaoh wanted the kingdom's masons to build his tomb, the masons were delivered immediately, for he wanted to see the pyramid ready in his lifetime. The Great Pyramid of Cheops, built over 4,500 years ago, employed 4,000 masons, who lived at its base in rows of barracks made from mud. These masons were *stonecutters*. Some of them "faced" the stone, that is, chiseled smooth the one side of the block that would show. Others cut out the blocks themselves, chopping them to regulation shape and size. The whole process of cutting and removing stone is called *quarrying*. The last part of the *quarrier*'s job—taking the blocks and lifting them into place—required armies of construction laborers. The average weight of a block in the Great Pyramid is two and a half tons. These blocks were moved without pulleys or wheels, for the Egyptians built pyramids with little more help than an ant colony has in building its hill. Skill was limited to the masons, the men who cut the rock; the others worked with nothing but their strength, and many lost their lives in the massive enterprise.

Egypt is full of forbidding stone monuments, for the priests built as well, raising temples while the pharaohs built pyramids. The priests were a wealthy and powerful caste. A census taken by Ramses III listed 900,000 workers owned by two temples in Thebes. Building temples provided constant work. Once a temple stood, it was not finished, but was continually being reworked. Teams of masons would demolish one of its wings for rebuilding. They would knock down walls, create great galleries, and then divide them. A temple fed on its own stone over decades.

Egypt's masons worked with granite, porphyry, sandstone, basalt, alabaster, and, the most common, limestone. This last was a favorite of the ancient world, with deposits scattered all along the shores of the Mediterranean. Masses of rock, just quarried from the earth, were split to a workable size with mallets of wood, crowbars, and bronze or copper chisels. The Egyptians could split two and a half tons of rock by their own strength alone. The masons started on the surface, working with their chisels and trying to drive cracks a few inches into the stone. Once the rock had been breached, they turned to their second method. A wooden wedge was jammed into the crack, doused with water, and left to expand overnight. It stretched the gap, sending faults farther underneath. Then the masons worked again with their chisels. They kept at the job, using first the chisel and then the wedges, and with these tools were able to break the stones for use.

After the first pyramid had been built, the pharaoh decided that stone was sacred, meant only for himself and the gods. This seems to have been a conservation measure: Egypt did not have much stone, and the throne's

Enslaved captives of war were often set to making bricks for early Egyptian structures. (From Egypt, *by Clara Erskine Clement, 1903)*

The stonemason uses a variety of tools to dress the stone and ready it for use in building structures. (By Jost Amman, from The Book of Trades, *late 16th century)*

appetite for it was very great. The priesthood laid its claim to most of what was left over; nobles could only buy stone in small quantities and at exorbitant prices. The pharaohs and the priests built what they wanted, and at the feet of these vast structures the rest of Egypt raised their homes. The commoners, by far the largest part of the population, lived in mud huts, which they built themselves. Masons built for the nobles, the few who could own slaves and build great houses. They followed the ruling elite's lead, imitating royal and priestly palaces and temples.

The masons owned by Egyptian nobles did some of the earliest bricklaying work. It was just as well that the pharaoh made stone so exclusive; the wealth it took to break, transport, and lift the huge stones into place was probably beyond even the aristocracy anyway. Wood was as rare as stone. Either might be used as the surface of a wall—always one conspicuously placed—but as nothing else.

Bricks, however, were as hard as rock, and much easier to obtain. They were made small—a worker could carry one in each hand—and came in roughly regular size and shape. The masons who used brick could build easily; the weight and strength of what they worked with were no longer obstacles to finishing a home. Masons stacked the bricks, carefully checking measurements and alignment, mortared the bricks (bound them together) with a mixture of dry mud reinforced with linen, and their job was done.

The bricks themselves were made from materials scooped out of the Nile; mud was mixed with chopped straw, separated into patties, and then left in the sun to dry. When kilns (ovens for drying or baking bricks and pottery) were introduced, many small brick-making establishments sprang up. Each one might employ fifty slaves, and each slave was expected to make two hundred bricks in a day. From spring to early autumn, one of these kiln groups could make up to a million bricks. Best of all, bricks were cool; stone stored heat, while bricks reflected it. In Egypt's climate, the ability of a building material to reflect heat was a major advantage.

Monumental stonework like that of the pyramids used no mortar; the blocks were cut to adhere to one another and were compressed together by their collective weight. The famous buildings of Greece, many of them erected in the several centuries before Christ, were more subtle in their architecture but were raised by essentially the same methods. The Parthenon of Athens has for over 2,000 years been praised for its beauty rather than its size, but it is a marvel as an engineering feat alone. It is composed of columns, pillars, and flagstones weighing a total of 20,000 tons and all resting in place by mutual tension. The demands of its architecture make its construction an even greater accomplishment than the building of the pyramids. Skilled Greek workers of this period cut blocks right at the quarry; a calculated layer of "fat"—that is, extra stone—would be left on, to allow for chipping while the stone was carted away. A mason might chisel his signature on a block that he thought he had cut with particular craft.

After several centuries of building on a large scale, the Greeks came up with a cement-like mixture called *mortar*, which was strong enough to hold stone against stone. In the second century B.C., crumbled rock was added to this mixture, and the resulting stronger mortar was the earliest *concrete*, which masons applied with a flat-faced tool called a *trowel*. The Romans introduced ash from their volcanoes to the compound. Their concrete was comparable in strength to the improved synthetic compounds used today. In the city of Rome itself, builders went so far as to fabricate entire walls of concrete—some of which still stand today—with rocks or baked clay fixed on as surfacing. These were easy to produce, providing one had the materials, and they transformed the process of building into a simple matter of arranging slabs into a system of walls, floors, and ceiling.

The brickmaker shapes and bakes bricks of clay sometimes mixed with hair or straw. (By Jost Amman, from The Book of Trades, *late 16th century)*

From the first century B.C. to the third century A.D., Rome had more money than any city in history had had before; Rome also had more masons, and their building never stopped. In Egypt and Greece, masons had raised monuments and palaces. Egyptian nobles had had houses of brick, while Greek homes, from whatever class, had been uniformly cramped and haphazard. In Rome, concrete walls allowed masons to work quickly and inexpensively, so they could house all the city's growing population. Roman emperor Caesar Augustus had ordered the disorderly slums of the city rebuilt; according to the chronicles, he found Rome "in brick and left her in marble"—or, to be more exact, durable lime plaster. By 350 A.D., an imperial census found that the masons had built 44,173 tenements or what we would call apartment buildings. Other classes had their own, far better buildings; the census listed 1,782 private homes in the city. These were generally made with stone foundations and brick walls, the rocks left rough and mortared together with a thick paste. The greatest nobles built structures as proof of what they could afford. During this period the typical atrium, or reception hall, constructed for a wealthy family's house tripled in height. One man paid 600,000 sesterces (about $50,400) for a marble bath. The historian Sallust claimed to have visited palaces as big as towns.

With this much wealth, projects could be begun and finished at whim. A story of feuding gentry in the countryside provides an example. A man invited his enemy to his estate for a few days' visit. The guest was surprised by his host's friendliness and generosity; the visit stretched out until, a week later, he set off for home. When he reached his own estate in the evening, so the story goes, he found his palace had been pulled down to the ground and the rubble carted into piles; a larger and grander palace now filled the site. According to the story, the man's old enemy had shown what he could do to punish—and also what he could do as a friend. No one ever quite believed the story, but its circulation gives a hint of what the Roman nobles' behavior must have been like.

Many Roman building workers, certainly the laborers who had to struggle with a palace's stone blocks, were slaves, the best of whom came from Greece. In Rome, however, skilled slaves could be freed by their masters and then have a chance of earning a living on their own; masons were no exception. Freedmen builders belonged to *collegia* (professional brotherhoods); masons and carpenters formed two of the earliest. (Builders who remained slaves imitated their more fortunate colleagues. The slaves of the Carrara quarries founded a *collegium* in 20 A.D.; four officers were elected each year.) Unlike other freedmen, though, a mason could not use his skills to set up a storefront business of his own; masonry, at least on the scale practiced in Rome, meant working as part of a team. A mason leased his services out to a building contractor.

Facts about masons who worked outside the Roman Empire during this period in history are few. In country after country, all that is left of the masons is their work, the structures they built. There are no surviving records of how these builders lived and worked. In many parts of the world—in North Africa, the Near East, and much of

These masons are working as a team to dress their materials and use them to build the large structure in the background. (From Diderot's Encyclopedia, *late 18th century)*

Asia—there were few masons, in any case, either because stone was not the preferred building material or because it was rare.

In China, for example, wood was much the preferred building material for structures; and over half of China's Great Wall was made of tamped earth, rather than stone. The eastern portion of the Wall—sometimes called "the great stone serpent"—is, however, testimony to the skill of the masons pressed into labor on the Chinese frontier. But because these workers were often outcasts of society—criminals, debtors, dissidents—and manual laborers at that, we know little about them or their methods of working. Tradition has it, however, that their close-fitting stonework results from an edict that any mason who left room for a nail to be driven between two stones would be beheaded.

Cambodia's jungles contain the city of Angkor Wat, made up only of monuments and tombs, covering several artificial hills built by unknown numbers of workmen in the 11th century, 700 years after Rome's fall. Scholars know something about King Suryarvarman, the man who ordered the building of Angkor Wat. But the names, dress, habits, methods, and lives of the people who carried out his orders are unknown to us.

Some masons specialize in exacting tilework, on floors and walls. (From Diderot's Encyclopedia, *late 18th century)*

We know just as little about the ancient civilizations in Central and South America. The Spanish and Portuguese invaders of the 16th century found wealthy peoples living in the jungles and mountains of the Americas. These peoples lived in magnificent stone cities, such as the Inca capital of Cuzco, with its stunning architecture formed from massive trapezoidal stone blocks. But the Europeans sacked these countries for their riches and settled down to several centuries of rule over the survivors. The stone cities are still there, but most of their history is gone.

In Central America, the Maya raised their great buildings from the ninth to the 11th century A.D., around the same time that the Cambodians were building Angkor Wat. The Mayan Empire rivaled the achievements of Rome, Greece, and Egypt, while using only tools made from stone. Although the Maya had a written language, calendars, and charts that listed the movements of the sun, moon, and stars, they never learned how to work metal. Masons built with granite, quartzite, limestone, and obsidian, and also fashioned from these the tools with which they worked. Like the Egyptians, they set wedges to split rock masses, though they also fell back on the technique of dropping slightly smaller rocks on the larger rocks that they wanted broken. They dressed the rocks with stone chisels that had themselves been dressed with smaller, sharper stone chisels. By these methods, the Maya built pyramids on the scale of Egypt's.

In Europe, masons were returning to work just as the Maya were about to decline. Barbarians had invaded Rome in the fifth century, sending Europe into the Dark Ages, brightened for the first time in the 11th century, with a revival of learning, trade, and skill. The Catholic Church raised churches and, more impressively, cathedrals, which were churches on a larger scale than Western Europe had yet seen. Their size and the daring of their architecture grew as the skill of their builders, over centuries, came to equal and then surpass those of ancient Greece and Rome. From 1050 to 1350, the French, the

most devoted of these builders, raised 80 cathedrals, at least 20,000 small village churches, and 500 greater churches. The cathedral at Amiens was built so it would be large enough for its clergy to hold one service for the whole population of the city: 10,000 people.

This is the best-known period in the mason's history. The cathedrals are Europe's pyramids. Their builders kept accounts on *fabric rolls*, six-foot scrolls scribbled full with figures. These records are not complete, but they provide information that earlier times cannot match.

The people on a masonry team specialized in different kinds of work, although the categories often overlapped. First, standing apart from those who worked beneath him, was the *master-mason*. Europe's great buildings were made from stone; any addition was trimming. A cathedral or castle stood if its builder could understand masonry; so all the *architects* and *contractors*, the men who designed an edifice and then saw that the workers carried out the designs, were masons.

The divisions below the master-mason were less definite; titles and sometimes even functions could slide

Tiles were made on a large scale in manufactories called tuileries. *(From Diderot's* Encyclopedia, *late 18th century)*

from one group to another. Roughly, masonry work was divided into *hewing* (cutting stone blocks) and *laying* them into place, or building with the blocks. A cathedral was not a building of straight simple lines; in thousands of places it was adorned with carved statuary and other decorations. Since the masons prepared the stone, they prepared these decorative items as well. Hewing extended up to delicate sculptural work, so it was thought the more demanding of the two categories. But it also reached down to *scrappling*, the roughest sort of dressing reserved for stones that would be out of sight, making up a wall's core. *Freemasons* carved decorations into the walls and fashioned elaborate ledges and pediments (the capping scrollwork of a pillar), using axes, chisels, and mallets. *Hardstone-masons* carved the statues, a job that demanded great skill. By the 13th century, some of the hardstone-masons had sharpened their talents to where they were known as *sculptors*, then more often called *imagers* or *imaginators*. They no longer worked as part of a masonry team, doing their part to complete a common building project; instead, they found buyers for their statues alone. *Roughmasons* primarily worked to put stones in place. They used a cord called a *plumb-line* to test true alignment of blocks. Their work shifted over into that of the bricklayers, a group not important in cathedral work; roughmasons and bricklayers sometimes shared the title *rowmasons*, a corruption of roughmason.

Other specialties were even less defined. A team building a cathedral was smaller than one might expect, perhaps only 30 or 40 workers. The cathedrals were immense, but they were built slowly, over a period of decades or even centuries. Still, even 30 or 40 people can perform a wide array of specialties among them. Some knew how to work marble and specialized in that; the *marble workers*, also called *marblers*, were probably an elite group, since the stone was expensive and hard to find. *Paviors* paved the cathedral's floors. One worker inspected each stone to see that its lines had been cut uniform with the line of the others. A *dresser* drew the designs for how the statues and embellishments should be carved, tracing on the stone itself outlines for larger projects, such as a central doorway or the front of a tomb.

Masons started work, according to an English chronicle of the time, "als erly als thai may see skillfully by day lahte," in other words, at daybreak. Work ended when the light was gone. A summer workday might last 16 hours. For darker seasons, the master-mason would on occasion order torches set up. In the building of England's York Minster, breakfast lasted twenty minutes and dinner an hour, with perhaps 10 minutes for an evening drink. The workers napped half an hour when the summer sun grew too hot. The masons took off days dedicated to favored saints, but received no pay for them; these came to about 30 holidays a year. Work at the site could not go on through the winter. That is why the men carving statuary back in a workshop, though paid much the same rates as the other masons, made much more money overall.

Masons wore special work clothes—aprons, clogs, tunics, and gloves (those who worked with mortar were in special need of gloves, to shield themselves from lime burns)—issued to them by the master-mason. He encouraged his men by paying bonuses for outstanding work, as well as buying the crew drinks now and then. He also took whatever steps he felt were necessary to keep the masons working hard. The masons who built Eton College could be fired for telling stories during the workday.

Masons on a job lived where they worked. Those who knew they would be able to hold onto their jobs summoned their families; they knew they would spend the rest of their lives within sight of the cathedral, for raising a cathedral often took generations. The project was so large that officers of the church paid out the money in installments over the years, with each generation paying for its share as the project went on. Even a modest-sized abbey might take 100 years to build. Building the cathedral at Exeter, in England, took over 200 years; the building was begun in 1112 and finished in 1369.

Not all the masons could settle permanently on the job site, however. The cathedral's patrons found these workers temporary housing. In a city, this meant an inn or a room in a private home. Outside the city, at a remote abbey in the country, for example, carpenters nailed together wood barracks for the masons.

Masons who did not have a project were forced to wander. No regular trade existed because only the most powerful—kings, the church, lords—had the money to build with stone. Masons had to keep moving, following gossip among their fellows until they found someone recruiting workers. Kings kept a few favored masons in permanent service; the rest, once their services could be dispensed with, were set loose again. Masons from northern Italy showed up in Spain's Catalonia; French masons journeyed as far as Uppsala, in Sweden. Traces of the same building styles appeared in country after country.

Masons grew to be free spirits. They waited centuries longer than most medieval trades to be regulated by membership in guilds. Their lack of organization might have put them at a disadvantage before their employers had not their skills been so valuable and scarce. Wages varied because they were set by bargaining between the builder and each of his workmen. Some masons could bargain hard. In 1415, William of Colchester, York Minster's master-builder, wrote to the King of England for protection from "stone-cutters, or masons" conspiring for his "death and ultimate destruction."

The trade gradually fell into its own sort of organization. At quarries and building sites, the masons had to have some place to retire for their meals and rests. Employers knocked together what came to be called *loges* (lodges); these were wall-less wood sheds that held 20 or so workers. These informal centers of friendship, discussion, and rule-making became, with the years, more formal meeting places. Newcomers came there to be trained; teams met after work to debate and decide upon the standards of the trade. With so many masons traveling

the countryside in search of work, a common set of rules was tested out and accepted by lodge after lodge. More important, one lodge knew the next and the one beyond it. A country's lodges shared a circulating membership; in effect, they made up a rolling, wandering club with hundreds of clubhouses. The masons' lodge became famous as an example of a successful cooperative network. Much later, in the 18th century, European idealists who called themselves Freemasons would create a semi-mystical society based on the model of the medieval masons' lodge. Even in the 20th century, many of the fraternal organizations that are so popular in North America, such as the Elks, still refer to their local organizations as "lodges," reflecting their inspiration from the masonic networks of medieval times.

The English masons codified their traditional rules in the *History and Articles of Masonry*, written down in 1430. The German masons followed suit in 1459. The Germans had the most cohesive of lodge networks; their rules mandated a system of regions, each with a lodge headquarters, and all acknowledging the Master of the

At the marbrerie, *blocks of marble are worked into suitable shape for use in building. (From Diderot's* Encyclopedia, *late 18th century)*

Strasbourg lodge as leader. Congresses of German masons convened in the 14th and 15th centuries, many of their delegates traveling hundreds of miles. English and German codes divided the craft of masonry into three grades: in English, *master*, *fellow*, and *apprentice*. A long list of rules was followed to select candidates for apprenticeship, and even higher standards were set for their training. Fines, fees, and the standards for entrance all kept rising over the years. The English and the Germans even wrote into their rules codes of etiquette for the lodge house, which would seem unbearably stiff if practiced today. From this time on, most drawings of masons show them in protective professional costumes of leather hats and thick aprons.

As the Middle Ages gradually gave way to the Renaissance, Europe became more prosperous. When many more people had money with which to build, on however small a scale, the job of the mason could not remain the same. Professional artisans, including the many kinds of builders, now wanted homes, not the huts that serfs had always lived in. The Ordinances of

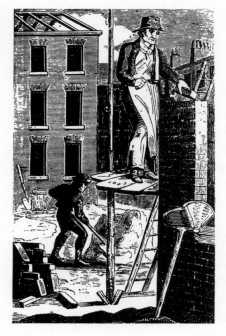

Though often dust-covered, 19th century bricklayers were often dressed in a jacket and long trousers, covered by an apron. (Authors' archives)

Worcester Guilds, issued in 1467, ordered all chimneys to be "of stone or *Bryke*." In just a few centuries, the great cities of Europe were rebuilt, expanding to many times their old size—and continuing to grow. Chamberlayne's *Angliae Notitia*, a survey of England in 1687, noted that "Houses in cities, that were heretofore usually of Wood, are now built of good stone or Brick...."

Masons no longer had to make their livings from projects that dominated the landscape; the scale of their projects shrank, as did the status of the patrons. The lesser gentry and merchants all wanted fine homes, and by the 17th century these accounted for more of the best masons' trade than did the demands of kings and high churchmen. Moreover, masons were actually making better livings doing smaller jobs. In 1603, the average pay of English masons was double what it had been between 1350 and 1500. By 1660, it was half again what it had been in 1603. This second increase came at a time when most workers' wages could not be expected to rise or even to keep pace with inflation. A fine mason, one who was as much an entrepreneur as a builder, could find himself even richer than the prople who sought his services. One Joshua Marshall, a royal mason in England, earned 46,000 pounds (about $575,000 today) in the last 10 years of his life.

The titles *rough-masons* and *imagers* no longer existed. Instead, *shopkeepers* and *statuaries* kept storefront workshops, employing their own teams of carvers; they prepared items of stonework, such as mantelpieces and headstones. *Overseers* contracted building projects. The building workers themselves were divided into apprentices and journeymen, who trained the apprentices. Young boys flocked to the building trade as apprentices. The overseer might hire out groups of them to help another firm on a project, adding to his own income. But many more wanted the career than succeeded in it; in 17th-century London, of the apprentices who began their seven years of training, over half would never become masons.

Errant stones of bricks from a mason's store have endangered more than one innocent onlooker. (Lustige Blatter)

Stone had long been the favorite material of masons, but brick was used for the smaller homes, and even for the walls of great mansions. Bricks were cheap, plentiful, and could be worked with easily; so buildings could be erected quickly and inexpensively, as the times demanded. Competing brickmakers used up much of the earth's clay, and, according to one newspaper, were tempted by secret additions of "the slop of the streets, ashes, scavenger's dirt." Many among the new crowds of houses fell down when their bricks crumbled. In 1744, an Act of Parliament allowed the London Brickmakers' Company to enforce standards for work. The Company decided not to, however, because demand for the cheap, poorly made bricks was still high.

Bricks were invaluable to England's North American colonies. Salem, Massachusetts, for example, had a brickyard as early as 1629. A Colonial home's foundation was made of stone, its chimney of brick, and its wooden walls faced with brick for insulation. A few decades later, settlements with more people and money could afford larger kilns and make even more bricks, relying less on the forests for building material. Bricklayers from the Netherlands arrived in Virginia, and within years had filled the colony's villages with brick houses. The core of Philadelphia, one of the greatest Colonial cities, was of brick, as were the mansions with which America rivaled Europe's builders in the 18th century.

The Book of Trades, an early 19th-century English compendium filled with practical information, tells about the workers of its day. According to information in this book, the jobs of masons and bricklayers had changed little over the previous century. Bricklayers of London, the book tells us, could insulate homes, make their chimneys and walls, and pave courtyards with bricks or tiles. "In the country," the book continues, "plaisterers' work is always joined to the business of a bricklayer, and not infrequently stonemasons' work also." Rural bricklayers also dug wells.

Bricklayers handled mortar with a small tool called a *trowel*, trimmed bricks with a *brick-axe* or sometimes a saw, and used "a stone" for polishing "when great exactness is required." The bricks they laid gave form to a house that had previously existed only on paper; they had to transfer the design to earth, using measuring tools to outline its distances and right angles. A line secured by pins was used to mark out where the rows of bricks would go. As a wall of bricks rose, a *level* was used to make sure that they stayed flat and in alignment. Laborers worked with the bricklayers, mixing mortar as called for and carrying it and the bricks in a *hod*, an open-ended basket fixed onto a staff (from which came the title *hod carrier*. A bricklayer could lay a thousand bricks in one workday. His fee was based on a certain rate for each 16 1/2 feet of bricks he laid; the laborer, on the other hand, was paid a flat salary, which usually came to roughly half the bricklayer's earnings.

Masons included *ornament carvers,* as well as *stonecutters,* the workers who hewed the rock out of the quarries. But for the building mason, or *stonemason,* the trade "consists in the art of hewing or squaring stones or marble; in cutting them for the purposes, and in being able to work them up with mortar." Stonemasons used much the same tools as bricklayers; they also used mallets, chisels, and saws. Great blocks of stone could be split into lengthwise slabs by a long saw, as large as a carpenter's pit saw but meant for one man; instead of cutting by teeth, the saw's weight, manipulated by the user, allowed it to bore into the rock. By this time even master-masons were workers, rather than architects or contractors. They charged for their work by the cubic foot. A master-mason earned about double the wage paid one of his journeyman helpers; these helpers earned slightly less than journeyman bricklayers.

From the end of the Middle Ages to the start of the 19th century, masons and bricklayers wore hats and sleeved waistcoats along with their aprons. But by the 19th century these had disappeared. Under their aprons, masons now wore shirts and jackets. A humorous English book of 1841, *The Heads of the People*, gives a description of a working builder: "His jacket of white flannel is powdered with the mingled dust of lime and brick; his stockings are white worsted, similarly spangled; his brogues [boots] guiltless of blacking...."

In *Under the Greenwood Tree*, published in 1872, Thomas Hardy had his own description of a mason from that period:

Being by trade a mason, he wore a long linen apron, reaching almost to his toes, corduroy breeches and gaiters, which, together with his boots, graduated in tints of whitish-brown by constant friction against lime and stone. He also wore a very stiff fustian coat, having folds at the elbows and shoulders as unvarying in their arrangement as those in a pair of bellows: the ridges and the projecting parts of the coat collectively exhibiting a shade different from that of the hollows, which were lined with small ditch-like accumulations of stone and mortar dust.

The extremely large side pockets sheltered beneath wide flaps, bulged out conversely whether empty or full; and as he was often engaged to work at buildings far away—his breakfast and dinners...he carried in these pockets.

Masons could expect to progress in the building trades from manual labor to architecture or contracting, but they remained artisans. Unlike most other trades, the building trades were relatively untouched by the new machines of the 19th century. The mason's position was not especially exalted because of this; in some parts of England and France, they worked hours comparable to those of the medieval cathedral builders.

Nineteenth-century masons did their work for contracting firms, taking assignments as handed down. The lodges belonged to a time long gone; now masons were among the first workers to fight for unions. They made their most important efforts early on and midway through the 19th century, when the pool of organized labor was still tiny. In the 1840's, the Operative Stonemasons' Society, with 4,953 members, was by far the largest union of any sort in Great Britain. It kept a list of "scabs," workers who took jobs vacated by their fellows who were on strike. The Society tried to pressure employers against accepting these men for any sort of work again, but in those days, the employers were still resistant.

The masons rebuilding Parliament went on strike in 1841, protesting treatment by their foreman. The contractors advertised for masons in other cities; one "society" sent a reply which began with this salutation: "To the Master Builders of the New Houses of Parliament, London. Gentlemen (miscalled)..." The strike lasted eight months before hard times—which workers then had to survive with nothing in the way of public aid and only meager resources of their own—choked it off. Throughout the century, times would stay hard. Charles Booth, an early sociologist who surveyed London and its workers in the 1890's, estimated that 49 percent of the city's masons and 55 percent of its bricklayers lived in poverty.

Like almost all manual labor, masonry has been transformed in the past century. After decades of fighting for economic security, masons found it; but technological change at last found its way to them as well. As for most artisans, technological change meant that some tool work was replaced by automatic machines. Rocks would come to be quarried with pneumatic drills, then sent through industrial mills. Machines would combine to transform them with grinding, planing, lathing, and polishing; the rocks would emerge ready for use, to be sent out to masons on the site. For masons, however, the materials themselves were first outmoded and then replaced; when that happened, masons saw most of their skilled work retreating into the factory. In 1824, Portland cement, derived from limestone and clay, was introduced. By mid-

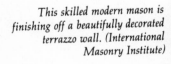

This skilled modern mason is finishing off a beautifully decorated terrazzo wall. (International Masonry Institute)

century, improvements made it popular across Europe. The ingredients allowed Portland to be almost as cheap as clay; its quality could be relied on, and it was far stronger than any lime mortar. This was the first modern concrete. Concrete had been unknown since Roman times, but 19th-century masons soon rediscovered its usefulness for buildings. Stone had never been able to bend under pressure; concrete, reinforced with a core of steel, could. Reinforced concrete became the favored material for building great edifices; the first entirely concrete skyscraper was raised in Cincinnati, Ohio, by 1903.

With the growing dominance of concrete, the cutting and placing of stones no longer counted as a distinct and honored trade. Only the maintenance of the old monuments demanded it; and this was increasingly done by people other than traditional masons. Today, some of England's young university students, wanting to make a career of work with their hands and enthralled by years of studying the medieval past, compete in seeking positions at one or another of the country's castles and cathedrals; they are hired to reface walls, carve replacement pediments, and search for quarries with appropriate stone. In the 1980's Leeds Castle employed Ted Filmer as its stonemason, under the Latin title *Magister Edwardus Cementarius* (Edward, Master Stoneworker). Although he has had no specific training for masonry work, Mr. Filmer does building and repair work acclaimed by expert architects, working without the aid of the mason's former technical helpers, such as *surveyors*. This sort of masonry work is preserved less by commercial need than by human fascination with stone.

For the millions of other masons at work, their jobs consist primarily of laying concrete blocks and walls in place. Almost all industrial buildings, many house foundations, and many houses in entirety, are of concrete. Stones and brick are used most often only for decorative facing. The work of the mason's hands is now restricted to carefully measuring where the blocks, concrete, or prepared rock should go, and then settling them there.

About 163,000 masons and bricklayers worked in the United States in 1980; bricklayers made up the greater percentage of that number. A quarter of all these workers are self-employed; these specialize in repair jobs and small-scale construction for homes, such as laying patios or building fireplaces. The International Union of Bricklayers and Allied Craftsmen sponsors an apprenticeship program; candidates spend three years of on-the-job supervision, along with many hours of classroom study each year. Many American bricklayers are of Italian ancestry, their forebears brought over the Atlantic in the early 20th century to build dams and large public buildings—continuing the centuries-old Roman tradition of stone-working.

For related occupations in this volume, *Builders*, see the following:
    Architects and Contractors
    Construction Laborers
    Plasterers and Other Finishing Workers

For related occupations in other volumes of the series, see the following:
in *Artists and Artisans* (to be published 1986):
    Sculptors
in *Manufacturers and Miners* (to be published Fall 1987):
    Miners and Quarriers
    Well-Diggers and Drillers

Plasterers and Other Finishing Workers

Once a building has been erected, the last step is to coat it, inside and out. This covering protects the building from the elements and can also be used as a surface for the addition of the building's decoration. Plasterers have not always worked on the outside of buildings, but they have almost always worked on interior walls.

The need for this sort of protection goes back to the earliest homes. Four thousand years ago, for example, the wood huts of Britain were sealed up with various pasty mixtures called *daub*, all of which relied heavily on mud; the daub was pressed into the cracks among a wall's trunks and branches. Primitive villagers found this a simple method of capturing heat and blocking off cold and wet; they applied the daub themselves, just as they had built their own homes. People in some parts of the world

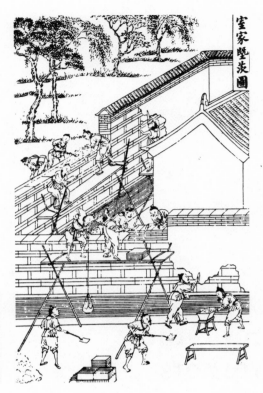

While bricklayers are building the basic structure, plasterers follow behind them finishing the outer surface. (From Chhin-Ting Shu Ching Thu Shuo, *imperial illustrated edition of the* Historical Classic, *1905)*

continue roughly the same pattern today. But richer nations raise up larger buildings, and the people who coat these form a profession of their own: the *plasterers.*

Plasterers worked throughout the ancient world. In Egypt, they were slaves who belonged to the pharaoh and his nobles, as did some other kinds of skilled building workers. In homes, they applied their plaster to wood partitions that divided the rooms. First, they bound together Nile reeds with rope to form a screen that covered the wood's surface; then they coated the screen with plaster. The plasterers also covered the long brick walls of corridors in the temples and pyramids; cracks and irregularities were covered up so that murals could be painted over a smooth surface.

The Greeks and Etruscans, in later years, followed similar methods. Although their plasterers were independent workers, their job remained much the same. Greek plasterers coated temples themselves, as did ancient Egyptian plasterers. Thousands of years after being built, the brick walls have crumbled away while the plaster goes on standing.

From the start, plasterwork has been of high quality. The Romans probably worked hardest at the trade. Like the Greeks, they used a sort of plaster called *stucco*, mixed from marble dust; the workers polished it so that it would shine like a mirror. Vitruvius, in his book *Architecture*, wrote more about plaster than anything else used in building. Apparently, the plaster had to be just right; all the details in the process of making it—materials, timing, motion—were listed meticulously.

The ingenuity of the ancient world largely created the craft as it would survive into this century. The first plaster, made in Egypt from burnt gypsum, was essentially the same as today's familiar *plaster of paris*. Moreover, the same tools of the trade are used today as were used in old Egypt, chief among them the trowel, a broad flat blade held by a handle. The plasterer held a lump of plaster on the trowel, spread the material on the wall with a brush, and then smoothed it flat against the wall with the trowel's surface.

Plasterers worked elsewhere beyond the Mediterranean as well, but few educated people took notice of their work. Plasterwork was being done in China by the time of the Han dynasty—roughly contemporary with the Roman Empire—and was widely used there throughout history. Plasterers were very often employed to cover rough brick-laid surfaces, which were then adorned with beautiful watercolor paintings called *frescoes*, many of which have survived in the dry parts of Central Asia. Because plasterers were manual laborers, however, China and most other Asian and African countries have few records of them and the way they lived and worked.

In Europe, the specialist plasterer vanished from view after Rome's fall in the fifth century A.D. Centuries passed before anything was built that required the skills of a plasterer. After the seventh century, some of the churches in England and France used rough plaster to disguise the bumps and cracks of their stonework. But even in the late 12th century, most homes still used the daub of ancient Britain.

Then, as Europe began to revive, more homes began to be built, and old trades revived, one of them being that of the plasterers. In 1212 when London was being rebuilt after a terrible fire, King John of England ordered all homes in the city to be covered with whitewash, a lime-and-water mixture that was painted on a structure for a fresh look, since it temporarily covered up many minor imperfections. The proclamation set pay for *whitewashers* and *mud daubers*; the daubers were now professionals who worked with a standard mixture of straw, mud, and clay. The whitewashers painted over both the daub and the house's wood frame.

The two professions worked side by side for a time, but as homes became less primitive and more comfortable, plastering began to replace wood daubing, until the older practice eventually died out. This change occurred first in the churches, where it became commonplace for walls to be plastered. In the Italy of the day, as in ancient Egypt, this plaster was meant as a surface for mural painting.

The first real homes to require interior and exterior work by plasterers were the mansions of the nobles. A contract from 1317 states that Adam, a plasterer of London, will use plaster of paris for both the inside and outside of Richmond Hall, belonging to Sir John de Bretagne, Earl of Richmond. This is one of the first written mentions of plaster of paris; the name is derived from the fact that the *gypsum* from which it is made was mined outside of Paris, processed, and then sold abroad.

Henry VII recognized the London Guild and Company of Plasterers in 1501, granting it "the right to search and try and make and exercise due search as well in, upon, and of all manner of stuff, touching the plasterers' work." The British in this period distinguished between rough and fine plaster workers. Plasterers did rough work, using a flat-faced tool called a *float* to smooth open

Whatever materials they use, roofers often work in teams. (From Diderot's Encyclopedia, *late 18th century*)

surfaces such as ceilings and floors; *pargetters* did more careful, delicate work, using the trowel on chimneys and in other such limited places. Plasterers worked with a variety of mixtures and different methods of decoration. A book written in 1519 noted that: "Some men will have their walls plastered, some pargetted and whytlymed, some rough caste, some pricked, some wrought with playster of Paris."

Renaissance plasterers learned from their Classical forebears. In 1518, Raphael, one of the most famous of Italy's painters, excavated Rome's Baths of Titus. These had been a showcase of ancient Rome's plaster ornamentation, and Renaissance artists were fascinated by them. Raphael's assistant, Giovannide Udine, experimented and at last reproduced the brilliantly white and hard Roman stucco. They used the material and the Roman plasterers' methods in a contemporary showcase, decorating the Loggia of the Vatican.

The Italians of the Renaissance were ready to consider plasterwork, like any craft, a potential art. Some sculptors seized on the new material, using it to model portrait busts; earlier, inferior varieties of stucco had been fit only for the reproductions sold to middle-class clients. Other craftsmen stayed more purely plasterers, doing architectural work like their predecessors, but aiming to create decorative art. A successful plasterer, such as Jacopo Sansovino of Venice, trained many followers; one of Sansovino's pupils was Vasari, a successful painter and the first biographer of Europe's new artists. In the early 16th century Francis I, king of France, wrote to the Duke of Mantua for the loan of some young painter and plasterer to decorate Fontainebleau. Whoever was the lucky craftsman selected, he was followed by many others; thus began the trek of Italian plasterers northward.

In the mid-16th century, an English plasterer, still a skilled workman and not an artist, earned almost twice as much per day as a carpenter or a painter. Henry VIII patronized some of the Italian emigrants, and their work pushed English plasterers to greater heights. The king's Nonesuch Palace showed to the fashionable what *pargetry*—which now meant decorative plasterwork—could do. One of the emigrants, the daughter of a man named Titziano Minio, became the only female plasterer we know of until the 20th century.

In this period, plasterers mixed sand, lime, and finely chopped hay; the combination was beaten until it became tough and resistant. The plasterers of Elizabethan times, at the end of the 16th century, introduced the use of molds for the more elaborate stucco work. First, the plasterers made the interior of the mold slick with soap or varnish; then they filled the mold with plaster and pressed it against the ceiling. Next, they pulled the mold away, leaving a new ornament on the ceiling. After waiting for the ornament to dry, plasterers, still working from a scaffold, carved the shape into finer detail, then polished it by hand. On their travels from job to job, plasterers carried their molds. Plasterers painted their work and sometimes even used gold plating, until the London Company of Painter-stainers, losing their trade in competition, petitioned Parliament to forbid the use of oil paints outside their craft. This step did not help the painters, however, for stucco whiteness quickly became the fashion.

The professional architects of the 17th century introduced their daring and extroverted sense of design, and the molded ornaments billowed out. During this time, plasterers worked only on the insides of buildings, producing ornaments for great houses and simpler work for more modest homes. A survey of English life published in 1697 claimed that "Houses in Cities...are now...cover'd with Slate or Tyle; the Rooms within...are ceiled with Plaister, excellent against the rage of fire, against the cold, and to hinder the passage of all dust and noise."

That sort of work was done by the lower ranks of the trade, who were now flourishing. The decorative plasterers, who worked for the rich, were not always allowed to plan their own work—that was the province of the architect—but the skill of their hands placed them very high in prestige. The best could reach a respected position in life. Near the end of the 18th century, a gentleman was showing some acquaintances around the lavish Academy Room at London's Somerset House. One of the guests related a story he had heard—that the man who had done the plaster for the room, working far overhead, had rolled off his scaffold and died. The surprised host then revealed to his friends that he himself had been the room's plasterer.

During the 19th century, the plasterer's work became much simpler; the trade contracted to the level we know today. From being something of an artist, the plasterer became solidly part of the working class. Plasterers worked for building firms, rather than for themselves. By the end of the century, British plasterers had unionized to protect their rights; one employer called them "probably the most impudent and independent class of men in the building trade."

In modern North America, simple flatwork is the standby of the plasterer, although a small market for decorative stucco still exists, especially among the

On high structures like cathedrals, steeplejacks had to develop various devices to reach the heights with some safety. (From Diderot's Encyclopedia, *late 18th century)*

affluent of California and the Southwest. Specialists called *lathers* generally put up the thin strips or sheets of material called *laths*; then the plasterers apply plaster, generally with a flat trowel, over this base. Of 24,000 plasterers in the United States perhaps 25 percent work for themselves; most of the rest are employed by *building contractors*. Union plasterers in the big cities earn a good deal more than other plasterers.

The plasterers have always faced competition from other finishing workers, artisans who add final touches to a building after its basic structure has been completed. It is these finishing workers who make a building "livable."

White lead paint had been made cheaply since the 17th century; beginning in the 18th century, some bridges and houses were painted rather than plastered or whitewashed; in the 19th century, painting became a commonplace way for coating most homes. *House painters* and *paperhangers* have now taken over a good deal of work that used to go to plasterers. Paint can protect the walls of a house against the weather; inside, it can provide both insulation and protection. Wallpaper is used to cover only the interior walls of a house; it serves just as decoration. Few workers practice both trades; most prefer to make a specialty of one or the other. There are about 382,000 house painters in the United States today, but only 21,000 paperhangers. A third of the painters and three-quarters of the paperhangers work for themselves, as independent contractors. They both earn the same average pay as plasterers.

Insulation workers, or *applicators*, have made a specialty out of one of the plasterer's old functions. They hunt out the gaps and cracks in a building's structure where heat can escape; these can be sealed with mesh, tape, or even a sprayed foam. This specialty took on new importance for Americans during the 1970's, when the cost of oil and gas for heating soared.

Roofers provide the covering for the top of a house. A roof requires much tougher material than plaster or paint. On the wooden base provided by *carpenters*, roofers first lay down a strong roofing paper, tacked together in sections. On top of this, they nail down the roofing materials, often shingles of asphalt or slate. The type of material used for roofing has varied widely over time and geography. In rural or jungle areas, where strong plant stalks, such as straw, reeds, or palm fronds are readily available, thatching has often been preferred for roof

Glaziers fit the panes of glass into windows for houses and other buildings. (From Diderot's Encyclopedia, *late 18th century)*

covering. The stalks are arranged on the roof in parallel, overlapping layers to form a mat that will shed rainwater. Where the soil is rocky, materials such as slate were generally preferred. Especially in earlier times, roofers were often known by the type of materials they used; so specialists might be called *thatchers* or *slaters*, for example. Today, *roofing contractors* hire out their workers for large building projects. However, 30 percent of all roofers work for themselves, and these do most of the roof-building and repair required by individual homeowners.

Glaziers are the people who fit panes of glass by hand into the window space of a wall. Most of their work comes from great construction projects, such as city office buildings. Modern glaziers work as a team, and a team may travel together from one building to the next.

Tilesetters have worked for thousands of years; their creations in the medieval Moslem kingdoms were elaborate and very beautiful. Today they do more practical work, laying down factory-made tiles of uniform size (squares that range from a half-inch to six inches along one side) and pasting them in place with materials like cement. The tilesetter's chief tool is a trowel with teeth cut in its edge; this both spreads the paste and cuts grooves that hold the tile in more securely. In private homes these tiles are generally used only in the bathroom. Tiles are used more widely in buildings where people work or learn rather than live, including office buildings, schools, and hospitals. Among the 20,000 tilesetters who work in the United States, the average hourly wage is slightly higher than the earnings of plasterers, house painters, paperhangers, and other finishing workers.

For related occupations in this volume, *Builders*, see the following:
Architects and Contractors
Carpenters
Masons

For related occupations in other volumes of the series, see the following:
in *Artists and Artisans* (to be published Fall 1986):
Painters
Potters
Sculptors
in *Manufacturers and Miners* (to be published Fall 1987):
Power and Fuel Merchants

Plumbers

People called *plumbers* have worked since the Middle
Ages, but plumbers did not specialize in water networks
until the 19th century, when enough buildings had
sanitation systems to make their servicing profitable.
Sanitation before that time was haphazard. In the
earliest villages, garbage and human waste were
shoveled into carts, to be wheeled away overland, often to
be used on farm fields as fertilizer. Flowing-water ditches,
dug through the streets, could get rid of waste after it had
traveled through a town's open air. But since the trenches
led to a river or lake, the village's water supply would also
be put at hazard. Many peoples—most notably the Hindus
of India and the Zoroastrians of Persia—placed taboos on
the pollution of rushing water.

Only a completely closed, artificially constructed system for waste removal could be trusted. Modern plumbers make their livings from the installation and servicing of such systems. Before these systems were invented and made practical on a large scale, however, through thousands of years when technology was limited, the practice of sanitation itself was looked on as a convenience rather than a necessity. Great nobles could command technology, and they reserved conveniences for themselves. About 2000 B.C., for example, when Minos, king of Crete (an island that is now part of Greece) built his palace, interconnecting pipes were built to pass behind the palace walls to carry away waste. Tanks released water that jetted through the pipes, washing the waste into underground sewers. Rainwater flushed these out, gradually. The royal family of Crete used toilets similar in make to those of today. But plumbers could not build a trade around the conveniences reserved for a few rulers.

Many early civilizations had bathrooms, like this Roman one, but little need for plumbers. (From Museum of Antiquity, *by L. W. Yaggy and T. L. Haines, 1882)*

Imperial Rome, 2,000 years later, built the greatest public water supply of the ancient world, constructing elevated channels called aqueducts along which the water would flow from country reservoirs to Rome. Thirteen aqueducts, one 14 miles long, carried fresh water to the city. The Romans also built bathhouses for the use of the public; in the fourth century A.D., the city had 11 such bathhouses.

The Baths of Caracalla covered ground six times larger in area than that of St. Paul's Cathedral in modern London. Over 850 private homes owned baths and many of the rich also owned flushing toilets. The wealthy could bribe workers to install surreptitious pipes leading from the public aqueducts to their private homes. Their toilets and baths were installed next to the kitchen, so that all the water used in the house would travel to the same spot. The Roman city of Timgad provided one public toilet for each 28 of its inhabitants. Apartment buildings for the lower classes might have one toilet on the first floor; for the poorest, public fountains provided water and public gutters places for disposal of waste.

Even this standard of water use could not be kept up after Rome's fall in the fifth century. King John of England, for example, bathed just once every three weeks. A palace would have one vast bath, its water supplied by servants with pails. All of a noble's honored guests would climb into the bath together while the water was still hot. In 1391, a *carter*, John Brown, brought an order of 229 pots of water to one castle. An English writer of that day considered the Danish very vain, noting that they "used to comb their hair every day, bathed every Saturday, often changed their clothes, and used many other such frivolous means of setting off the beauty of their persons." Public bathhouses operated in many medieval European cities, though they had scandalous reputations and were often simply glorified brothels.

Plans still exist of the Christchurch Monastery, located in Canterbury, England, and its private water system. The system was very elaborate, and worked quite well in supplying the kitchen, baths, and latrines. In 1349, inhabitants of the monastery were among the few people in England to be left untouched by the plague epidemic called the Black Death. A 15th-century Portuguese nobleman built a castle with a similar system of pipes and toilet drains, flushed by running rainwater. There was enough work of this sort for a new kind of *plumber* to take it on as a specialized part of his trade. Medieval plumbers were people who worked with lead. Their work included roofing and fashioning embellishments for walls and ceilings; some even prepared coffins. The process of melting ingots, working them into pipes, and then installing the pipes for an occasional abbot or noble was only a small part of the medieval plumber's work. But it was also the part that demanded the most skill and brought the best rewards. When the Ordinances of English Plumbers set payments for the trade in 1365, installing pipes was assigned twice as much pay as roof work.

Toilets remained a rarity late into the 18th century. England's Queen Anne, in the first decade of the century, used at Windsor "a little place of Easement of marble with sluices of water to wash all down." But in mid-century, Keddleston, a great country manor, had only one toilet for its hundreds of rooms.

William Paul Gerhard, a *sanitary engineer*, wrote in 1899 of what life had been like a century before:

> The houses were low, dark, ill-ventilated...and often full of foul air....Cesspools were commonly located underneath the houses, or placed in the ill-aired courts in the rear...[In the streets] crevices of pavements retained the solid filth, while the liquid soaked into the ground and contaminated the public wells.

All the water used in a house was carried in buckets from these wells.

At the end of the 18th century, English improvement of valves made possible the first toilets that could be safely counted on to flush. Joseph Graham, one of the inventors,

Throughout the world, water carriers have operated to bring water to city-dwellers wherever no public water systems were available. (From Picturesque Palestine)

made 6,000 toilets between 1778 and 1797. By 1814, a writer of the day mentioned toilets as standard fixtures of the better homes. Families in England's richer city neighborhoods could have water piped into their homes from the public supply, though only for a few hours a day. Domestic plumbing could still be primitive, even dangerous, in its construction. One widely circulated anecdote told of two workers nearly killed by an explosion of trapped gases; they had been examining a leaky pipe by candlelight.

Sewers originally were built to drain storm rains from the streets. Although waste found its way into them as well, an old London law forbade the entry of "fecal matters" into the city sewers; this law was changed only in 1847. The old law still held in Paris and Baltimore in 1899. England introduced the first sewers using pipes rather than flowing water courses. Its sewers released into the Thames, which then carried waste back to the city, where, Joseph Graham writes, it "oscillated to and fro." From 1850 to 1875, Sir Joseph Bazalgette constructed an entire sewage-removal system safely underground; it carried waste 14 miles beyond London Bridge.

When this still did not give complete security, the city spent $750,000 a year on treating its sewage by chemical processing, to lessen the danger of disease.

In 1800 the United States contained only five public waterworks. By 1851, the number had increased to 68; by 1897, it was 3,196. The cities of Europe also took their model from London. Graham claimed that "all central water-works systems originated practically since 1850." The people of the 19th century built these water systems because both water and human waste had to be removed from the open air; the first could become contaminated, and the second could contaminate. As late as 1871, Edward, England's Prince of Wales, could and did catch typhoid after a visit to a noble friend's home. The national scandal was followed by determination on the part of the public to ensure safe and clean drains. Edward remarked, in a publicity coup, that if he had not been prince, he would have been a plumber.

The people who specialized in constructing the necessary waterworks, however, did not approve of the title *plumber*. They saw themselves as *sanitary engineers*, freeing humankind from disease. The sanitary engineer Gerhard once referred to his old mentor's "noble enthusiasm for sanitation." Today, human waste is often to many people a joke; but a hundred years ago it was a horror that caused widespread disease and death—as it still is in many undeveloped parts of the world. Graham remarked that "the details of drainage, ventilation, water-supply...and general sanitation, and the installation of sanitary appliances are now in many cases entrusted to sanitary engineers who make a specialty of domestic engineering."

Working plumbers without such exalted aims found their realm—sanitation for buildings—contested in these early days by the sanitary engineer. In 1877, a lecturer at the New York City Lyceum of Natural History claimed that any installation for the home should be performed by a sanitary engineer, as "the practical plumber" was "generally ignorant" of the job's safety necessities.

The plumbers spoke back. Steven Hellyer, a leader of the trade, addressed colleagues gathered in the London hall of the Royal Society of Arts: "Lying there in those strong arms of yours, slumbering in the hardened muscles, resting in the well-trained fingers and educated hands, lies the health of this leviathan city!" His firm, Dent and Hellyer, issued its employees an elaborate document certifying, in part, that the bearer was "a Skilled Artisan, and a good Sanitary Plumber."

By the 1880's, English houses were routinely built to include toilets, and the plumbers practiced a flourishing trade. In 1837, English plumbers worked 54 hours a week, including Saturday; by 1873, their workweek had increased to over 58 hours and their pay was up by a third. Some even complained about the widespread installation of plumbing. The New York City Lyceum's lecturer remarked unfavorably upon the proliferation of toilets in city dwellings, noting that directing the flow of water and waste to and from so many individual points caused the plumbing systems to coil and complicate themselves dangerously. He blamed this on the desire for "luxury" and, more important, "the ingenuity of the mechanic in increasing expenses...." He was not alone in making the complaint. By 1896, the average plumber's pay in England was almost twice what it had been in 1837.

The plumber's work was far from easy, however. A manual published in 1874, Dr. T. Pridgin Teale's *Pictorial Guide to Domestic Sanitary Defects*, gives an idea of what the Victorian plumber faced in his work. The pipes in a house could be rotted through ("crumbled like shortcake"), and basement cesspools were often full of rats. On repairs, the plumber often had to smell the source of trouble, learning to distinguish scents from one another. Teale noted: "Neither are all dangerous smells of a foul nature, as there is a close, sweet smell which is even worse." The plumber might sometimes flush oil of peppermint down the drain and sniff where it emerged. Some bought "Drain Grenades" or "Pain's Drain Rockets" to release smoke through the pipes. Once exploring a

house's woodwork, the plumber was sometimes expected to do other jobs there as well, such as installing bells for the larger establishments, the wires for which traveled alongside the pipes.

Today a plumber works on every sort of house-fitting that deals with water or waste—from garbage disposal units to showers. He or she works with several sets of tools. Rules, steel tapes, and squares, all in different sizes, are used for measurement and for laying out plans for work. To check the proper placement of pipes, the plumber uses a *level*. This tool consists of a bar containing three connected vials, each with a bubble; the bubbles right themselves as the pipes approach correct alignment. The *plumb bob*, a weight attached to a long cord, is dropped down vertical pipes to locate their center, and follow it from one floor of a house to the next. A compass and dividers are used to measure where to cut pipes. A variety of saws are employed to cut through walls or other parts of the structure to allow installations, while chisels are used to alter the pipes themselves. The plumber uses both a hand-turned mechanical *pipe cutter*, and a more powerful *soil pipe cutter* that is chain-operated. A variety of wrenches are used to grip pipes with different surfaces; the *strap wrench*, for example, wraps around polished chrome pipes that must not be scratched.

In large-scale construction, a *plumbing contractor* is hired to lay in pipes for a full-sized building. The plumbing system itself is designed by the building's architects, with advice from engineers. The chief engineer approves the plumbing contractor's plans for work. The plumbing contractor directs other plumbers, those for sewerage, water, and gas systems; and also the *steam fitters*, who lay systems meant only to carry high-temperature water and steam. This last is used either for heating or in industrial processes. Some plumbers specialize as *estimators* employed by general building contractors. When a contractor needs expert opinions in order to gauge the bid for a job, the plumbing estimator is asked to figure out how much money the plumbing for a project will cost.

A plumber may work as the employee of a plumbing contractor or of a more general building form. Some plumbers serve as *public health inspectors* for the government, or as wholesalers of plumbing supplies to plumbers' firms and retail stores.

Large cities have apprentice committees staffed by both the unions and the contractors; they select apprenticeship candidates, set programs of training, and assess the apprentices' progress. An apprentice must be at least 18 years old; he or she is expected to complete five years of supervised on-the-job training, along with classroom study under a master plumber. Students are taught useful chemistry and physics, government regulations applying to sanitation, and how to read and draft blueprints. The apprentice must pass a state examination to gain a license. After apprenticeship comes status as a *journeyman*; then the plumber can work without supervision. A journeyman of five or more years' standing can take a second examination, and qualify as a *master*. This allows him or her to work as a plumbing contractor.

In 1980, 470,000 plumbers were at work in the United States; of these, 10 percent were self-employed. The plumbers and steam fitters belong to the United Association of Journeymen and Apprentices of the Plumbers and Pipe-fitters Industry of the United States and Canada. Masters are not included in the union, because they are plumbing contractors and, consequently, employers.

For related occupations in this volume, *Builders*, see the following:
    Architects and Contractors
    Construction Laborers
    Plasterers and Other Finishing Workers

For related occupations in other volumes of the series, see the following:
in *Helpers and Aides* (to be published Spring 1987):
    Bath Workers
    Movers
    Sanitation Workers
in *Scientists and Technologists* (to be published Spring 1988):
    Engineers
in *Restaurateurs and Innkeepers* (to be published Spring 1988):
    Costermongers and Grocers

Roadbuilders

Roadbuilding involves the planning and design of roads by *civil* or *military engineers*, the supervision of construction crews by *overseers,* and the actual building of the roads by *construction laborers*. In early civilizations these roles were often blurred, although the vast majority of the manual labor force was made up of slaves and war captives. Earlier, in prehistoric times, traders had carved out long-distance routes through the wilderness and across deserts; several thousand years B.C. some of them built log roads, called *corduroy roads*, through swampy sections. But roadbuilding as a profession did not emerge until the rise of the great civilizations and empires of the ancient world. They made organized efforts to construct roads not only for trade but also, and more important, for military mobility. Good roads also made it easier for tax collectors to reach the far reaches of the empire and thus exercise some amount of control over the people who lived there. Roadbuilders, then, were very important to ancient governments.

Roadbuilding has always required the combined efforts of technical engineers and laboring construction crews. Early civilizations had very few engineers who specialized in roadbuilding as compared with, say, tunneling, marsh draining, or building construction. Still, the great roads built in antiquity were projects that took many years and demanded the long-term, close supervision of engineers who came to stake their reputations more on roadbuilding than on any of their other efforts. Military engineers were the main roadbuilders, since the movement of troops and supplies preoccupied the minds and monies of rulers in a time of almost endless wars, rebellions, and campaigns of conquest.

Much of the actual labor was typically done by slaves, although major roads required so much labor that many farmers and other laborers also had to be pressed into such service; soldiers were also set to work building roads, especially those that had strategic military significance. Commoners often paid their taxes or fulfilled other obligations to the central government through roadwork assignments. This system of labor as payment to society or government is known as the *corvée*, and it was used to get roads built right up to the 19th century in most of the civilized world, and is still used today in some of the less developed countries. Convict labor has also been a time-honored method of filling the ranks of roadbuilders. Even petty crimes were often punishable by this manner. Whatever the source of labor, few ancient or medieval road construction crews included paid—and hence "professional" (in the strictest sense)—laborers.

Little is known of the development of roadbuilding in ancient Asia, but the discovery of an extremely advanced system of brick-paved city roads in the culture of Harappa and Mohenjo-Daro in the Indus Valley indicates that roadbuilding must have made great strides there 5,000 years ago. Engineers there even provided for curved corners, which were a relatively late development in the West, since they were only made necessary by a regularly heavy flow of wheeled traffic. Chinese rulers and the later Mauryan rulers of India appointed a regular civil officer to supervise the construction and maintenance of roads. But the art was not highly developed; most roads were really only shored-up dirt paths. Exceptions to this rule were the Chinese trestle roads, akin to those built to carry railroads through the American Rockies in the 19th century. As early as the third century B.C., engineers employed by the central Chinese government surveyed, laid out, and constructed wooden roads—balconies built out from or hung on bolts from rock faces—through mountains and gorges. They continued this tradition up to modern times. In the same period, peoples on the west coast of South America were building causeways—raised roadways across swamps—and cutting step roads out of sheer rock in the Andes; the roads they made would form the basis for the later, more famous Inca roads that Europeans found when they arrived in the Americas. We do not know how the early roads were built, or by whom; but in later Inca times, a clan or tribe was moved to the

For thousands of years, people have built corduory roads of logs through marshy areas, as here in northern Canada. (Royal Ontario Museum, Sigmund Samuel Gallery)

In many wooded mountain areas, as in China and later North America, wooden trestle roads were built, like those that would later carry railroads. (From Picturesque America, *by W. C. Bryant, 1872)*

local area and given charge of building and maintaining a certain section of the highway.

The first specialized road engineers may have been the *ummani*, the pioneer corps of the army of the Assyrian king Tiglath-pileser I around 1100 B.C.; they cleared paths and constructed crude roads before the advancement of troops. Especially close attention was paid to the building of royal roads leading to the king's palace. One such avenue for Sanherib of Nineveh in about 700 B.C. was 90 feet wide and lined with imposing pillars. Severe penalties were prescribed for anyone misusing the road or encroaching upon it with any structure—even an overhanging balcony. The construction crews for such projects labored under severe conditions for long hours in the desert suns or marshy swamps. Besides digging and hauling dirt and stones for the project, they were saddled with the back-breaking job of crushing rocks, stones, clay, and pottery bits until they formed a relatively smooth and impermeable road surface. Sometimes such debris was burned in place to help it "melt" into the subsurface layer of clay or dirt.

Perhaps the greatest chapter in roadbuilding history was written by the Romans. Famed for their technical expertise and practical genius, they constructed highways that lasted for centuries, some even up to this very day. The vast network of Roman roads served medieval and even modern builders in outlining the most appropriate routes for parallel or sometimes coinciding works. The Roman *surveyor* designed these routes over mountains, around marshes, and through forests with such cunning that, for centuries, they were accepted and used as the only ways to go. The subsurface construction of the Roman roads was so solid that later engineers merely had to repave the surfaces in order to render them useful, even for the heavier carriages and carts of later times.

The Roman surveyor and engineer of roadways was usually a military officer serving the army or appointed to civilian projects by the government. He worked without stock patterns and made every project its own unique work of art, taking into account the variable environmental factors such as terrain and groundwater. Many roads connecting small towns were nothing but dirt paths (*viae vicinales*). The *viae publicae* (public roads) were usually the best constructed, as they were financed and maintained by the state. Appius Claudius, one of the earliest engineers of roads, persuaded the Senate to allow him to build a highway from Rome to Capua; this was the famous "queen of roads"—the Via Appia, or Appian Way. So wonderful was the job he did that his family erected a shrine to him along the roadway. It soon became a tradition for well-known Romans to have shrines built for themselves alongside great roads. Of course, in order to be so honored one usually must have had an important role in the building of the road—either as an engineer who designed and built it, a politician or ruler who approved it and allocated public funds toward the project, or a private individual who donated considerable sums of money for its construction.

Roadbuilding in Rome became a common way for politicians and senators to win popularity. An imperial board of *highway curators* was appointed to see to the building of roads. Besides approving legislation for public road projects to be financed by the government, these officials also put their own money into such ventures. Those who held public office in distant territories of the empire or in rural communities often won votes by promising to get roads built and sometimes were legally bound by the very terms of their office to contribute financially to roadbuilding projects. Rome was a thriving civilization, with armies and traders constantly on the move throughout the empire. Roadbuilders played an integral role in the growth of Roman society, in the expansion of the Empire's borders, and in the strength of the government's administration of that Empire. It is no wonder that politicians and engineers who contributed to the construction of highways and roadways scored high in public approval and were often eulogized and immortalized as heroes for their work.

The great Roman roadbuilders left a legacy to their modern heirs, most notably in the building of bridges and causeways. (From Diderot's Encyclopedia, *late 18th century)*

The construction workers themselves enjoyed none of this glory. They labored tirelessly, digging ditches up to 3

feet deep to lay the firm rock foundations that Roman engineers became famous for. Earlier engineers had simply pounded stones into the soft dirt or clay, but their work was constantly being damaged by ground erosion. Roman construction teams took far greater pains to make roads that would not easily wash away. After the ditches were dug, they were filled with stones and broken pieces of pottery or brick. This layer was finally surfaced with heavy stones or hexagonal (six-sided) blocks of volcanic rock. There was a fairly well-developed division of labor. There were *foundation crews*, who dug the foundations; *pavement crews*, who applied the final road surface; and *clearance crews*, who drained marshes, pulled roots, and cut down forests to make way for the roads. These laborers were joined by skilled and sometimes paid *masons*, who specialized in cutting milestones and engraving them with the proper mileage and the names and accomplishments of emperors, generals, and the like.

The construction crews often worked under inhuman pressure and suffered unimaginable hardships in different areas of the far-flung Roman Empire. They had to clear tree trunks, level sand dunes, drain surface oil slicks (in North Africa), haul heavy loads of stone, cut forests (especially in Britain), and drain marshes. In Rome itself, slaves provided a good portion of the labor for these construction crews, but elsewhere the work gangs were composed mostly of farmers and other citizens, who were typically forced into such service. Whether road workers were elite engineers and surveyors, skilled masons or lowly laborers, all were subjected to common hazards, especially outside Rome. In Africa, many died in sudden floods or were killed by wild beasts. There and elsewhere, they were subject to raids from unquiet tribes while working in recently conquered territories. Troops frequently had to stand guard to protect construction gangs, and forts were sometimes built alongside worksites.

Despite all the hazards and pitfalls of ancient roadbuilding, the Romans were the best in the profession for many centuries to come. Considering the fact that Roman engineers and surveyors had no compasses, maps, or other technical and mathematical aids, some believe that they were the most accomplished builders ever. One thing seems certain: they stand among the most efficient and practical in the business of constructing roads. The surveyors were ingenious in finding the shortest and easiest route between two locations, and the engineers often performed near miracles in sticking to the surveyor's guidelines. They built bridges across rivers, tunnels under harbors, and bridges spanning mountains; they drained marshes and cut through rocky hills. They thought of every practical measure in such constructions. The military surveyors and engineers who were lent out for civil projects, for instance, saw to it that major highways in distant parts of the Empire such as Britain or Gaul were flanked on both sides with deep trenches or high embankments. This arrangement would break the momentum of chariot raids against Roman troops moving along the roadway, and provide the ambushed foot soldiers with something to crouch in or behind for protection. For the same reasons, many roads were lined with trees or pillars. The laborers performed superhuman feats of hauling, digging, and crushing, while working constantly in conditions that cost a great many of them their lives. All this resulted not only in the finest roads in antiquity, but ones that would be copied and followed for more than a thousand years thereafter. The leaders of the roadbuilding profession gained great respect during this period, but shortly after the fall of the Empire their profession fell into nearly total obscurity.

The Middle Ages featured weak political control and only the occasional rise to power of any central authorities or administrations. Since the long-distance Roman roads traveled through countless small and hostile kingdoms, they were only spottily and sporadically maintained. They ceased to exist—for administrative purposes—as whole roads, but only as segments of roads: the Florentine segment, the Frankish segment, and so

forth. Many governments and feudal lords charged taxes and tolls for the use of the roads, but these monies were typically considered as sources of revenue to be used for almost anything *except* the maintenance or construction of roadways. Travelers and traders paid constantly increasing tolls to take roads whose physical conditions steadily deteriorated. Moreover, the medieval highways were plagued by robbers and bandits who went virtually unchecked—there being no national military units or laws, and no police protection. It is often argued that road maintenance, construction, and safety were not very important in an era when there was not enough trading activity (and virtually no pleasure traveling or tourism) to warrant such government involvement and expenditures. On the other hand, if roads had been better maintained and guarded, perhaps trade and communication would have improved. Those who did work on repairing and occasionally building medieval roads were usually peasants obliged to work for their landed lord without pay. Their reward for such service was the lord's protection and the right to live on his land and till his earth for their own subsistence. Western culture became a rural society after the decline of the Roman Empire. Peasant road crews were employed mainly to see that the roads were cleared of such things as fallen trees, vegetation, and mounds of cow dung (the roads were commonly used for the movement of animal herds), so that farm produce could be readily transported—and so that the lords and kings, along with their troops and messengers, could travel with relative ease. It was not until the 10th century A.D. that actual road construction was begun again, and much later than that before it gained enough importance to stimulate the renewal of roadbuilding as a professional activity.

During this long period of neglect of European roadways, the Chinese were making progress in the field. In their attempts to unite a massive and widely dispersed empire, Chinese emperors employed civil engineers and military personnel in large numbers to build an elaborate network of roads.

The Commercial Revolution, lasting roughly from the 16th to 18th centuries, marked the renewal of the roadbuilding profession in the West. It was during this time that the greatest modern advances were made in roadbuilding technology. Interest in such activity was spurred, of course, by the renewal of large-scale trading activity. For many years this activity had had to be carried on along water routes, because of the dangers of road travel and the state of disrepair in which most inland routes stood. Private entrepreneurs were more likely to pour money into building canals than roads because canals could be limited to specific uses, and afforded greater speed and carrying capacity. Many mining companies, for instance, built canals to carry metals and coal from the pits to the foundries and factories where they could be used. Because such a canal was privately built, the builder of the canal could control access to it and reserve it for his own private use. It was very difficult to reserve a roadway for such a limited private use, and the heavy traffic on roads required upkeep and repairs that private companies did not wish to be responsible for. Besides, barges were faster and carried heavier and larger loads than rickety and clumsy wagons bouncing over rocky and rutted roads.

By the 17th century, most roadways were used by mail carriers, packhorses, and herds of animals being driven to city butcheries. In Britain, each individual parish was charged with clearing and maintaining a section of the "king's highway," which consisted of the main routes connecting the kingdom. Each parish appointed a "surveyor of highways" to take charge of this responsibility. He was largely ineffective, though, as he was unpaid and held office (usually reluctantly) for only a one-year term. Moreover, roadwork was done mostly by paid labor by that time, and it was simply too costly an undertaking for most towns to bear.

During the 17th and 18th centuries in England, thousands of laws were passed by Parliament in an attempt to make roads more uniform and provide for more regular maintenance of them. However, these complicated and often conflicting laws provided little incentive for professional roadbuilders. Before these professionals could get to work building roads, they first had to unravel a mass of confusing legal entanglements. The first group to do so were the private *turnpike trusts*. These private groups of investors were granted 21-year terms during which they were authorized to take over the chore of roadbuilding and maintenance for a parish. In return, they could collect tolls. The first turnpike built under this arrangement was the one connecting London and York, completed in 1663. By the 1800's Britain had some 20,000 miles of turnpike roads.

Thomas Telford and John McAdam, meanwhile, were establishing roadbuilding as a specialized scientific profession. Telford, known as the "colossus of roads," first worked on canals in the second half of the 18th century. One of the few "surveyors of highways" who took his appointment seriously, he built roads with deep foundations and adequate drainage to prevent landslips. He also paved them with finely graded stones, which iron-shod horses would pulverize and pack together, in an attempt to prevent the holes and fissures generally caused by rainwater. Older roadways had been drastically *cambered* (pitched high in the center) to allow for water runoff. While this cambering helped with drainage, it

made travel very treacherous, for wagons would commonly tip over. In order to keep their wagons upright, drivers were forced to ride the center of the road, a practice that resulted in excessive wear of the road's peak and that led to many a brutal battle for right of way, since only one wagon could pass at a time. Telford provided proper drainage under the road so that only very slight cambering was necessary; as a result, roads were rendered considerably more usable. As one of the first great roadbuilders of modern times, Telford became so famous that the landlord at his rooming house in the Salopian Coffee House at Charing Cross had to build more rooms to keep up with the increased business that the master attracted. When given notice of Telford's departure, he exclaimed: "What, leave the house! Why, sir, I have just paid 750 pounds for you!"

John McAdam, a commissioner of highways in Scotland and later Bristol, England, also took his job seriously. He refined a system of working a water-tight binding medium into the pavement so that the underlying construction did not have to be so deep or elaborate. This new process made roadbuilding much more cost-efficient and earned McAdam considerable income as a private consultant to various turnpike trusts.

Despite the technical advances made by Telford, McAdam, and others, however, roadbuilding was still a labor-intensive process, that is, a project that required a very large labor force, and since labor without slavery or corvée systems was costly, so was road construction. The British government had no desire to spend money on such works, especially since it was surrounded by some of the best natural waterways in the world. Besides, because public police forces were not yet trusted in a nation where people remained suspicious of central authority, road travel remained relatively dangerous in England for many years.

While the British were responsible for important technical contributions to roadbuilding, the French actually built more roads. Henry IV had appointed a *Grand Voyer* to centralize roads as early as the 16th century, and Louis XIV made the task of organizing the nation's roadways one of his pet projects. The French were

After the late 19th century, newer, smoother surfaces were commonly laid with rollers, in place of the old cobblestones. (From Harper's Weekly, *September 18, 1869)*

the first to make roadworks the responsibility of the national government, and in 1716 the Department of Bridges and Roads (*Ponts et Chaussées*) was established to fulfill that responsibility. French roadbuilders received great social esteem and recognition, and the profession became an honorable and elite one in their hands. Pierre-Marie-Jerome Tresaguet, whose scientific contributions to the field rivaled those of Telford and McAdam, grew wealthy through his work. In 1747 the first college of road engineering was founded in France. By the time Napoleon rose to power, the Corps of Roads, Bridges, and Highways had over 200 engineers and inspectors, who had been given considerable authority and liberal financial support to weld the French empire with an advanced network of roadways. As the democratic revolution approached, the policy of corvée had to be dropped and road laborers began to receive pay for their work. This development made roadbuilding more expensive and slowed down the process until Napoleon came to power and used his military forces to construct some of the most remarkable roads ever. These roads were not built without their own, often tragic, costs, however. The engineers of the Grand Armée saw at least 400 and perhaps as many as 700 construction workers killed by rockslips, landslides, and work-cradle crashes while they were building the highly acclaimed Simplon Road in the Swiss Alps. Napoleon eventually restored the corvée by giving it a different name—the *prestation en nature*.

In other parts of the world, roadbuilding lagged as a profession. In Germany travelers often preferred muddy fields to the rocky, rutted, and flooded roadways. American "trail blazers" merely cleared forest-ways and widened old Native American paths or moved westward. As people pushed across North America more roads were built through the thick forests and treacherous mountains. Hostile Native Americans and disease-laden mosquitoes posed constant threats to the laboring crews as well as the on-site engineers and surveyors. These dangers slowed down the process of roadbuilding in the

West considerably. Most of the roads in the East were built, paved, and maintained by private turnpike trusts after 1785, but in the West roads were frequently just rough pathways. During the great Gold Rush of the 1850's the westward trails were extended into the Rocky Mountains. The "builder" of one section of western road, "Uncle" Richard Wooton, was an old trapper who suddenly found himself taking in some $5,000 a year in tolls. Some of the routes were so treacherous that wagons had to be lowered down mountain passes with ropes.

The 19th century saw the growth of great interest in inland travel, for the newly industrialized countries had to move goods, products, and raw materials to the new factories and cities. Travel was becoming more common and tourism fashionable. Yet roadbuilding was not profoundly affected by these changes at first, mostly because of the superiority of canal and especially railroad transport. It was the rising popularity of wheeled vehicles toward the end of the century that finally made more and better roads necessary. One of the first effective lobbies for public roads was the Road Improvement Association, a group of British bicyclists who banded together in 1886. In the United States, Colonel Albert Pope of the Hartford and Columbia bicycle firm petitioned the government for better roads and persuaded authorities at the Massachusetts Institute of Technology to advance special lectures on road engineering. In England, a national road administrative board was founded in 1909—the first national roadbuilding authority in the United Kingdom since the days of the Roman Empire. Automobile manufacturers joined the bicycling lobbies as governments in France, England, America, and elsewhere began to respond to the demand for better roads. The advent of the automobile and the rise of the trucking industry made roadbuilding and maintenance major occupations of the 20th century.

Along with the sudden need for more roads came an increase in the mechanization of road construction. Toward the end of the 19th century, the *pavier* had become a highly skilled artisan, adept at selecting and fitting the elements of the road surface. *Ditchdiggers* worked long hours at hard labor, but also earned an honest day's pay to provide for their families. (A great deal of this labor was also provided by convicts working in chain-gangs.) Today roadbuilding requires fewer workers. Paving is done by mechanized pavers. Scraping machines loosen the earth, while bulldozers remove it for digging, trenching, and landscaping. While the use of road construction labor has declined since World War II, the machines that have replaced the workers are expensive and their operators must be skilled and therefore well trained and well paid. Moreover, modern urban road systems include a great many elevated roads, so that even greater skill and more sophisticated machinery are called for. Even the raw construction of roadbuilding now demands relatively skilled technical workers. Their efforts, though, are generally unheralded, even if well rewarded financially.

Roadbuilding today involves the efforts of specialized surveyors, engineers, and designers to plan routes that are not only cost-efficient but also as useful and durable as possible. It is often a frustrating task of balancing material and labor costs within national or local government budgets, while also considering traffic use and convenience. Special *traffic engineers* must come up with specifications and designs that take into account traffic volume, headway clearances, gradients, curvatures, and many other practical considerations. At the same time, *landscape engineers*, especially in Japan and America, concentrate on design elements that emphasize beauty and soil retention. In many countries, such as China and Russia, military and political factors weigh heavily in roadbuilding plans.

In any part of the world, roadbuilders must also consider a maze of private, public, local, federal, and state landowning and land-usage laws and rights. As a result, roadbuilders must exercise considerable diplomacy, skill, and patience in performing their work, on the engineering, planning, and design levels.

For related occupations in this volume, *Builders*, see the following:
    Architects and Contractors
    Construction Laborers
    Masons

For related occupations in other volumes of the series, see the following:
in *Communicators* (to be published Fall 1986):
    Messengers and Couriers
in *Harvesters* (to be published Spring 1987):
    Farmers
in *Leaders and lawyers*:
    Political Leaders
    in *Manufacturers and Miners* (to be published Fall 1987):
    Miners and Quarriers
in *Scientists and Technologists* (to be published Spring 1988):
    Engineers
in *Warriors and Adventurers* (to be published Spring 1988):
    Soldiers

Shipwrights

The first vessel people made to travel on water was probably the *dugout*. In its simplest form, the dugout is a log burned and gouged until it is hollow enough for a person to sit in, though some early dugouts seem to have been far more elaborate than that. Any civilization that existed near trees and water had both the makings for dugouts and the incentive to build them. Some peoples went on to devise other kinds of vessels; others made additions and improvements to the old style until the craft could leave the rivers and coasts to cross the open sea.

The people of the South Pacific islands made very sophisticated, seaworthy dugouts. The Maori of New Zealand, for example, continued making dugouts until the beginning of this century, and a British observer was able to record their methods. The boats they built were meant for ocean voyages, and in this sense might qualify as what Westerners mean by *ships*. A builder wandered the island's forests, inspecting the strongest trees. The one chosen had to be chopped down and then carried to the shore, no matter what its size or what the distance. The log could be immense; many of the Maori boats were 70 feet long. The branches were trimmed off and the bark stripped. Then the remaining trunk was worked down with torches and stone tools. With the trunk lying flat on the ground, the workers leveled off the top half of the log and then drew the outlines of the dugout, which resembled a canoe. They followed these lines as they hollowed out the log. The dugout's walls were strengthened with extra wood so it could stand up to travel over the seas: the builders chopped out beams called *gunwales* and lashed them along the length of the interior of the dugout to provide bracing against the waves. These modern Maori dugouts were clearly very sophisticated survivors of a very old boat-building tradition.

The first fully carpentered boats, so far as we know, were the galleys of early Egypt, which were powered by crews of rowers, although sails were used as well. The shape of the hull or body with its rounded bottom and its pointed ends—the prow in front and the stern behind—apparently stayed much the same from 3000 B.C.

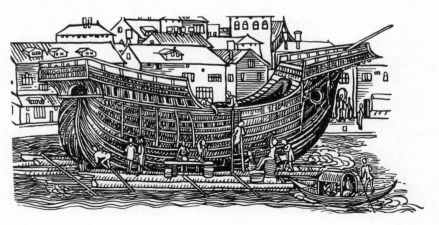

Venetian shipbuilders are working on a raft floating on the water. (From Journey to the Holy Land, *Bernhard Breidenback, 1486)*

until the fifth century B.C. Although Egyptian shipwrights did some building with wood, Egypt had few forests, so they had to find a more readily available material that was still light enough to float on water. The answer, as so often in ancient Egypt, was papyrus, a tall water plant that the Egyptians also used to make paper. Papyrus reeds that grew along the river could be reaped with a scythe and then tightly bound together to resemble logs or woven into sail and rope. The earliest vessels with mast and sail were used only to travel the Nile, being too small and not nearly strong enough for an ocean voyage.

Figurines found in tombs from 2000 B.C. show some Egyptian shipwrights at work. They are *carpenters* building boats from wood, a precious commodity, generally imported. The *keel* plank was the boat's central shaft, which balanced the boat on the water; all other pieces were built onto the keel. Two rows of ribs, curved and upright, made a frame. When the frame was complete, the carpenters worked in teams to saw planks four inches thick; these were laid on the frame with edge touching edge. The carpenters did not have nails; instead, they affixed the planks to the frame with broad and round wooden pins called *dowels*. These techniques appeared earliest in Egypt; they appeared again in India, Persia, and a half dozen other early civilizations.

Shipwrights coated the hulls with pitch and melted wax; all gaps were sealed up tight to keep out water. The ships were made narrow so that they could slice through the waters. Early galleys were moved by rowing; the distances they traveled required many rowers, pulling on long oars. Sails stayed simple: there was a single mast at the ship's center with a square of canvas or papyrus to catch the wind. But before such boats could survive long voyages on the open seas, they had to be strengthened. At first, to shake off shocks from the ocean, Egyptian ships were built with hulls that could be adjusted. A rope ran along the center from *bow* (front) to *stern* (back). When the rope was tightened, the hull drew in to become more compact. But a single strong wave could still send a bulge up along the hull's bottom. The Mediterranean peoples learned to fight strength with strength; like the Maori, they slid long gunwales along the ribs of their ships.

The Phoenicians, living in cities along the coast of what is now Lebanon, invented the *round ship*, whose hull was shaped like a broad oval bowl. These relied on their sails, rather than massed oars, to send them forward; a small crew could manage them, and at the same time the hull could carry far more goods than could be stored in a galley. The Phoenicians became great traders, possibly reaching even as far as Britain to buy tin.

The Greeks, too, are remembered as great shipbuilders; their ships carried colonists all around the Mediterranean. A Greek city, Corinth, claimed a shipbuilder as one of its legendary heroes. The Greeks did not follow the Phoenicians in building round-hulled ships; instead they built larger galleys, with greater concentration of power in their oars. Galleys stretched from 100 to 150 feet long; width went to 20 feet. The galleys carried enough men to row two, three, later even four or five banks of oars. The Greeks aimed at the greatest size that could still be managed with efficiency. Equipped with brass beaks at the prow, their galleys became warships; a captain treated his ship as a weapon, aiming it at another and then sending it hurtling forward. With luck, size, and skill, a Greek warship could split an enemy in two.

Specialized *architects* designed and oversaw the building of Greek ships. Their work was big business in the coastal cities, where people made their living from trade. At least 57 of these *master shipwrights* lived in Athens from 360 to 320 B.C.; probably there were 30 working in the city during any single year of this time. A shipwright ran a dockyard rather than the ordinary artisan's workshop; many different kinds of workers were needed to handle such huge projects. The remains of Greek ships show carpentry as painstaking as that which went into cabinets; craft was expected. Like most Greek crafts, shipbuilding continued down family lines; the necessary skills were passed on from father to son. Pheneklos, a shipbuilder mentioned by Homer, for example, was the son and grandson of carpenters.

A contemporary account describes the work of a builder named Hiero from Syracuse, a Greek colony in Sicily. Hiero was "eager to gain a reputation in shipbuilding," so he built several grain-carriers, on a huge scale. He had wood "enough to build sixty *quadriremes* [four-banked galleys]," brought from Italy and Spain, "hemp and pitch" brought "from the Rhone Valley" in southern France, "and the rest of his needs from a variety of places." All in all, Hiero hired 300 artisans, not counting *construction laborers* and assistants.

Hiero then found "carpenters and other craftsmen, chose one...to be foreman, and gave the project his personal attention daily." One ship took a year to be finished. Its hull was at last nailed together with copper spikes, each one weighing at least 10 pounds. Inside, the ship was built with three levels of cabins. The floor was done in mosaic tile, picturing scenes from the *Iliad*. The top level housed a gymnasium, "marvelously flourishing plant beds," and so on. Horses could be kept in the hold's 10 stables. This story demonstrates that the Greeks, with the devotion of enough money, could produce the equivalent of a modern ocean liner.

Carthage, a North African colony of the Phoenicians, was a leader in Western Mediterranean trade. The city could stay rich only so long as it had a fleet without rivals, so shipbuilders won public honors. Carthage's ships were probably the best of the age, though Carthaginian shipbuilders continued to use old methods and did not even use nails until the third century B.C. But Carthage had the misfortune to run up against the ambitions of Rome. The early Romans were landlubbers, but good at taking others' ideas and developing them. A Carthaginian ship—so the story goes—beached on Italy's coast. Roman carpenters took it apart and learned how to put together a second one. To this they added a *corvus*, or boarding ramp; at sea, Roman ships would drift as close as possible to the Carthaginians. Next, the Romans would flip the boarding ramp of their ship until it stuck into the shell of the Carthaginian ship; then Roman soldiers would march across the ramp and board their enemy's ship. The trick turned each naval battle into a land battle—at which the Romans excelled.

By the first century A.D., Rome's empire enclosed the Mediterranean. The navy had shipyards of its own, and merchants maintained ones almost as large. As trade grew, so did the size of ships. The ships that carried grain to the Romans were built to carry 250 tons. From the fourth century B.C. to the fourth century A.D., Mediterranean ships, whether Greek, Carthaginian, or Roman, were meticulously constructed, regardless of size. A Roman river boat found at the bottom of England's Thames River in 1910 gives us evidence of these careful construction techniques. Its boards were laid edge to edge, fastened with dowels. The frame was made of many small ribs, spaced about a foot apart.

After the fall of Rome, however, almost all the secrets of technology and craft were lost. The Romans had learned to use iron nails, but now, when these could be found at all, they simply pinned planking to the frame rather than joining the planking itself more tightly together. Planks were laid to overlap rather than from edge to edge. The frames, hacked out from logs, became massive, each beam widely spaced from the others.

The ships of the Dark Ages were narrow, open galleys like those of 3,000 years before. The Vikings of Scandinavia, in Europe's extreme north, built their first *nydam boat* in the fourth century A.D. A sail was added in the sixth century, but oars kept the nydam moving. It was made narrow and long; the first ones had room for 14 rowers along each side. The shipwrights fashioned these boats from *clinker boards*, boards that were fastened so that they overlapped. By the eighth century, these boats had left Scandinavia's shorelines and become seagoing ships; the Vikings traveled in them to loot and terrorize nations in many parts of Europe. The nydams of that time could carry good-sized squadrons. The Vikings measured their ships by the *rum*, the space taken by a pair of rowers seated side by side. The first nydam measured seven rum; those in the eighth and ninth centuries could be as large as 40 rum; 30 rum became the average.

In the oceans off southern Asia, other mariners—and shipbuilders—had been sailing for thousands of years. The countries around the Persian Gulf and the Red Sea had virtually no wood of their own, so they had to import wood, generally either from Lebanon on the east coast of the Mediterranean or from India, which had fine hardwoods resistant to the rot of tropical waters. With little in the way of natural metals, Arabian shipbuilders developed a boat that was sewn together with heavy fiber ropes, rather than nailed together. With these ships, Arabian mariners sailed to and settled along the coast of Africa; later, they developed even larger sewn ships that they sailed routinely to China on merchant ventures.

The Chinese themselves had a long and creditable history in the shipbuilding art, though in some periods they withdrew from the sea. Chinese shipbuilders had

Supposedly the building of Noah's Ark, this actually shows shipbuilding methods in the early 16th century. (Engraving by Stradamus, from National Maritime Museum, Greenwich)

little status, because they were considered manual laborers, so their work and lives are not documented as well as some other aspects of Chinese life have been. Although shipbuilders worked to specifications as to type and size of craft and although these specifications could be especially detailed if the vessels were for imperial use, they did not work from blueprints or plans. Instead they depended on the experienced eye and skill of the master-shipwright in charge of the project. Some of the builders did, however, make models of the ships to be built; the Chinese account *Chin Shih*, written around 1158 A.D., notes of shipwright Chang Chung-Yen:

When they began to build ships, the artisans did not know how. So Chung-Yen made with his own hands a small boat several [tens of] inches long. He called it his "demonstration model." Then the astonished artisans showed him the greatest respect. Such was his intelligence and skill.

At around the same time, another Chinese shipwright used models to help in estimating costs, as recorded in the *Sung Shih*:

When he [Chang Hsueh] was Prefect of Chuchow, he wished to construct a large ship, but his advisers were not able to estimate the cost. He therefore showed them how to make a small model vessel, and then its dimensions were multiplied by ten [so the cost of the full-sized ship] was successfully estimated.

Chinese ships were built in various styles, among them the *junk*; this flat-bottomed boat had a high deck and distinctive sails, with strips of wood inserted into thin pockets at intervals, to hold the sails flat. With their well-known ingenuity, Chinese shipwrights made a number of remarkable innovations, among them the development of the magnetic compass and of the watertight compartment, word of which was brought back to Europe by Marco Polo.

The shipbuilders with the longest tradition on mainland Asia, however, were the Indians. Indian sailors had been traveling the Indian Ocean, both east and west, for many centuries B.C. and over the ages had developed considerable shipbuilding skill. A thousand years before Marco Polo, a Chinese writer described a "people who lived to the south...[who] rig their ships...with as many as four sails, which are arranged...fore and aft...there are trees with leaves more than a yard long. These are woven together for making the sails. The four sails...are placed slantingly to receive the wind...The wind...is thus cast back from one sail to the next, so that they all benefit from the propelling force." One sail did not have to catch all the wind's force, with the risk of being snapped, so "the worry from too tall a rig is removed." The Indian ships could travel "without avoiding gales, which makes very quick passage possible." After a ship had been away for a voyage of a year or more, Indian shipbuilders took it in for repairs and overhauling. They sealed its hull with a fresh layer of planking, adding on to the two already in place. A ship that accumulated six new "skins" was usually retired.

In the 13th century Marco Polo brought back to Europe news of shipbuilders' accomplishments in the East. He saw ships made in India that required "a crew of 300 men....The ships carry as many as 10 small boats." As late as the 18th century, an Englishman would write of Bombay that "the natives...build incomparably the best ships in the world for duration...even to 1,000 tons and upwards," adding that the Indians "excel in the art of building ships."

In Marco Polo's homeland of Italy, the traders still traveled the Mediterranean in galleys; only the most daring left the Mediterranean and crawled along Europe's Atlantic coast as far north as the Netherlands. In 1268, King Louis IX of France commanded his shipwrights to build ships 110 feet long, each one able to carry 50 horses in its hold. This was an outstanding achievement for medieval shipbuilding. Aside from a nation's king, however, few people had the money to pay for building a ship—and few people were able to specialize as shipbuilders.

But new developments were on the way. Apparently by random trial rather than by any study of design, the shipbuilders of Portugal developed a round-bottomed sailing ship, which they called a *caravel*. It used three masts, two of them square-rigged, like those of northern Europe; the square sails could catch the wind directly and provide the force needed to speed the boat along. The third mast was *lateen-rigged*, like those of the Mediterranean galleys. This meant the sail was a triangle set at a 45-degree angle to the mast. The combination of sails allowed a captain to manipulate the wind's force without having to wait and hope for a favorable breeze to set the craft going. As the Phoenicians had done long before, the Portuguese abandoned their oars and broadened their boats; ships could again leave the shoreline.

The caravel itself did not last long; it was copied and then surpassed. In the 16th century, the Spanish *galleon*, sailing with four masts, became the finest craft on European waters. Trade and military strength could be won by ships; each power wanted the best. Technical development, though haphazard, followed. "Clinker-building" was gradually abandoned by shipwrights around the mid-15th century; an English government report declared *clenchers (clinker-builders)* to be "feeble, old and out of fashion."

In 1512, Henry VIII appointed Sir Edward Howard to build a navy for England. Sir Edward imported his shipwrights from Italy. A contemporary source claims "the fame of Genoa and Venice [two of Italy's great maritime trading cities], long the envy of Europe, passed quickly to the shores of Britain." This was not quite the case, but England had at least made a start. The best shipwrights the crown could find were put on pay for life, to be called upon when needed.

As is the case with all kinds of artisans, shipwrights were not all equally skilled. A 1495 Act of Parliament classed shipbuilders, in descending rank, as *master-*

This early 19th-century shipwright is uniformed in an old-style sailor suit. (From Phillips' Book of Trades, *1823)*

shipwrights (sometimes called *master-carpenters*), *hewers*, and *able clinchers*. There were also *master-caulkers* and *mean caulkers*; they sealed up seams and crevices in the ship's hull. Caulkers gave the final touch to what shipwrights had built and did not rank with them in respect; a master-caulker earned, by law, only as much as a hewer.

European shipbuilders generally used the same basic tools. A French print from 1580 shows shipwrights at work. They use an *adze* (an axe whose blade curves in and then out, used for shaping wood surfaces), a *cross-cut saw* built for two men, *spikes* and *mallets*, and chisels and axes for shaping the logs into beams.

Europe's shipbuilders, once their trade had revived, built ships that could cross oceans. Following the lead of Christopher Columbus, mariners regularly made trans-Atlantic voyages. Traveling the coasts of the New World, they met craft of a quite different sort. An early captain, Christopher Hall, recorded his first meeting with Eskimos. His ship had sailed into icy waters when it was met by a silent group of small, dark men, each one floating before the ship in his own boat, a *kayak*. "Their boates are made all of seales skinnes, with a keele of wood within the skin...[the boats] be flat in the bottome, and sharpe at both ends." Each Eskimo lived and traveled in his own kayak; when invited to board the ship, they carried their kayaks on their backs.

Somewhat later, a missionary named Hans Egede reported on the *umiak* of Greenland, another boat sewn from skins rather than cut from wood. Unlike kayaks, however, umiaks could be 60 feet long. They were "large and open, like our Boats...and these are called Kone-Boats, that is, Women's Boats." The women rowed them. Men thought it "unbecoming...to row such a boat....And when they first set out for the Whale-fishing, the men sit in a very negligent Posture." The boats could "also carry sails, made of the Bowels and Entrails of Seals...and with these Sails they sail well enough with the Wind, not otherwise."

Back in England, shipwrights won their first charter for a guild in 1604. The number of shipwrights multiplied as the trade grew, though many were not specialists. Many kinds of artisans took part in building a ship; during the 17th and 18th century, scholars estimate, only 40 percent of the workers involved in building ships were actually specialists in marine construction.

By the 17th century, respectable treatises on the science of ship construction were being written in France, Sweden, Russia, and Spain. In 1681, Louis XIV's minister, Colbert, issued the first code of rules to demand more scientifically efficient ship design. Conferences of scientists met in Paris to discuss the use of geometry in shaping the ship's hull in such a way as to overcome the resistance of the water. English writers of the 17th century remarked on the superior design of French ships.

However, the English may have overestimated their rivals. A writer in the French city of Toulon noted, "It cannot be denied that the art of constructing ships, so necessary to the state, is the least perfect of all the arts."

Not much of the scientists' research had reached even "the best constructors," who worked "almost entirely by the eye...the same constructor building at the same time two ships after the same model most frequently makes them [with]...quite opposite qualities." The French shipwrights often worked from plans, but the plans were not based on knowledge. The writer underlined his point: *"It is not yet known what the sea requires."* The result was that "Chance has so much to do with construction, that the ships that are built with the greatest care are commonly the worst."

At least, however, someone was in charge of the ship's shape and construction, an artisan having taken on the job of deciding how a ship should be put together, even though he did not fully understand the craft. Master-shipwrights managed dockyards, or shipyards, where the ships were built; they decided what the ships would be like. They administered pay, food, and shelter to their builders while the work was being done; they also maintained the docks and warehouses. In addition they visited forests to select which trees should be felled for shipbuilding. From 1500 to 1700, the details of a ship's construction increasingly came to be planned out on paper by the master shipwright before building was begun.

The master-shipwright's earnings were generally double the pay of the best artisan employed at the yard. In 1695, the master shipwright of England's Portsmouth dockyard made 200 pounds (about $2,400 today). Master-shipwrights would supplement their income by taking on apprentices. It became customary for apprentices to master geometry and principles of structural design; such study was not advanced, but at least a tradition was being built. Shipbuilding techniques, once developed, were kept secret from other builders, and were often passed on from generation to generation within a family.

The earliest of the master-shipwrights drew their artisans from among the lesser group of *boatwrights*. But increased demand over the decades meant adding more

and more workers to the team. A complaint of the 1570's about all these half-trained workers has been preserved in print: "their manners are mutinous." In 1693, the building of one ship for England's navy required 10 land carpenters, 30 general laborers, 4 caulkers, 12 timber hewers, 28 sawyers to produce planks, and 50 men who specialized in fashioning the ship's pieces and fitting them together.

In Europe, the master-shipwright of a royal dockyard worked under officers appointed by the throne, taking orders from above and then managing the details of how they would be carried out. If the dockyard was private, the master-shipwright probably owned it. The royal dockyards had money; their work was slowed down by corruption, but the designs used for ships could show a high degree of skill and training. The shipwrights of the private dockyards more often worked fast and by formula. Private shipbuilders started work when they had a contract in hand. The master shipwright bargained with each artisan hired, paying either day by day or a flat fee for a job, specified by contract. Craft techniques changed slowly, and a children's reference book, *The Book of Trades*, published in England in 1804, gives a good idea of how the shipwrights worked: "in a dockyard...six or eight men, called quartermen, are frequently intrusted to build a ship, and engage to perform the business for a certain sum, under the inspection of the master-builder. These employ other men under them, who, according to their contracts will earn from fifteen or twenty shillings to two or three pounds per week."

Master-shipwrights did not expect to get rich; their business depended on too many factors that were unreliable. It took more than a year for an ordinary merchant ship to be built; half of this time was spent in negotiating for labor and wood. Artisans and laborers traveled from one dockyard to another; they might work on merchant ships or for the navy, depending on where a job fell open. At one time or another, the master-shipwright had to find *plumbers*, *glaziers*, *joiners*, *coopers*, and *carvers*.

According to *The Book of Trades*, a ship, while being built, rested on "solid blocks of timber placed at equal distances from and parallel to each other." This arrangement of blocks was known as the *berth*. The book describes the shipbuilding process as follows: "The first piece of timber laid upon the blocks is generally the *keel*, which, at one end, is let into the *stern-post*, and at the other into the *stem*." The stem was "a circular piece of timber in the front; into this the sides of the ship are inserted."

William Sutherland, whose *The Shipbuilder's Assistant* was published in 1711, tells a good deal about the work of 18th-century shipbuilders. "I cannot tell," he wrote, "whether the Saw or the Augre [a sort of drill, which bored holes through which wedges could be driven, binding together the hull] is the most necessary Instrument." The two-man cross-cut saw was still essential; it had largely replaced the axe and *addice* (adze) for the job of cutting apart timber. Large axes were used for shaping. Nails that ranged in size from heavy spikes on down held the planking together. Oak, the strongest wood in Europe, was the shipwright's favorite.

Sutherland intended his *Assistant* as the textbook that would bring order to a confused field; he thought that "by clear and demonstrable Rules" shipbuilding could "be reduced to certain principles...as any other art whatever." A shipwright's learning, he thought, ought to comprise a half dozen disciplines: "Arithmetic, Geometry, with the Knowledge of the Laws of Motion [physics], and the different increase between Rest and the Greatest Motion, as also how Bodies gravitate; and to order the Equipping [of a ship], the Experience whereof is the noblest part, without which all the rest would be but insignificant." Sutherland expected a lot of anyone who tried to build ships: an understanding both of the laws of design, and of what could or could not survive at sea. "But he that has acquir'd both the Theory and Practice," he concluded, "makes an accomplished Shipwright!"

Sutherland claimed to find "a Crowd of good Artificers" among his colleagues, but he acknowledged that there was no way of sifting out the unskilled. Shipbuilding was "counted a very vulgar Imploy; and which a man of very indifferent qualifications may be Master of...." Sutherland had his standards, and the craft he practiced would probably have been better off if it had adopted them, but this would not happen for a long time. Meanwhile a prospective shipwright learned whatever he did by experience and by apprenticeship to a master. The master could teach his apprentice anything he liked—or nothing at all—depending to some extent on how good a contract the boy's family had been able to negotiate. No standards were set by guild or government. The master might take on an apprentice only as a way of turning a profit. After two years in a dockyard, an apprentice could be hired out as an assistant to a ship's carpenter, in which case he had to send his earnings to his master for the remaining five years of his apprenticeship. When the full seven years had passed, the apprentice graduated to journeyman, his training having accumulated quite haphazardly. Journeymen, and even apprentices, often wandered from their home regions to pose as qualified shipwrights, without bothering to join a guild.

England's North American Colonies set no time limit on a shipwright's apprenticeship. The average fell somewhere between four and seven years. Towns often indentured their orphans to shipwrights just to make sure that the orphan's lodging would not be at public expense. The Colonies had too few shipbuilders, so the masters could demand high pay even for an apprentice's work.

The launching of a big ship—here the Maine *at Brooklyn Navy Yard— is always cause for celebration. (By J. O. Davidson, from* Harper's Weekly, *November 29, 1890)*

That pay went to the master; one such master made almost as much from his apprentice's work as he did from his own. Most apprentices came from the families of workers or farmers; they expected to earn a living, not to win a fortune. Shipbuilding apprentices from more prosperous families often planned to become merchants, expecting that shipbuilding knowledge would give them an edge over future business rivals.

An American journeyman could convert himself into a master as soon as he had the money to buy land for a shipyard. There were no guilds in America, and the land came cheap. The shipwright needed a plot of land on the water that was not pitched too steeply. Skilled labor had to live nearby, so small cities and towns were preferred; in larger cities, land was too expensive for most shipwrights. The American shipwright generally could not afford more than six workers at a time; the workers preferred to be paid by each piece they delivered; that way they could move among several projects at the same time. The early Philadelphia tax records gave an average assessment to shipwrights that was lower than that of bakers, carpenters, hatters, tailors, and bricklayers. Shipwrights in smaller towns made more money, but the most successful would take their capital and stake it on careers as merchants or planters. Only then did they win what they considered real success.

In 1806, England's Commission of Naval Revision found that the Navy's designers and shipwrights "were...sadly ignorant of the theory of naval architecture and lacking in general education." At this time England had the best fleet in the world. *The Book of Trades*, published two years before the Commission's report, voices a contrary view, more hopeful than true. "Shipbuilding is to this country one of the most important arts; it is studied as a science by the learned, who denominate its *naval architecture*." Perhaps the best that can be said is that the first steps toward such a science had been taken. A School of Naval Architecture was founded near the Portsmouth dockyards in 1811. It closed 21 years later,

Today shipwrights work with massive marine gas turbines, which drive modern passenger and cargo ships. (United Technologies Corp., from The American Society of Mechanical Engineers)

however, having graduated 40 students, each one rejected for jobs by the Admiralty and Navy Boards.

Outside such short-lived academies, designers continued to build a science by experiment. The nations of Europe now traded all over the world. Chinese tea could be harvested only in the summer. European merchants all wanted their ships to be the first to get to China for the harvest and the first to get back with the freshest leaves; great fortunes could be won by the race—so great fortunes were spent on designing a ship that would win.

Robert Fulton's *steamship*, the *Clermont*, had sailed up the Hudson in 1807, but steam power was still thought too dangerous. Ship design, in the words of *The Book of Trades*, meant only giving "a proper shape to the bottom of the ship." Shipwrights proved their design skills by coming up with the *clipper ship*, a sailing ship that for 30 years held off competition from steam. The first clipper ship was launched from Baltimore, Maryland in 1833. Its builders wanted it to carry as much sail as possible, with the absolute minimum of hull to resist the water. It was V-shaped in the prow, U-shaped in the stern. One clipper, the *Rainbow*, sailed from New York to Canton, China and back in six months and fourteen days—a record. From 1840 to 1860, American shipwrights turned out one clipper after another; to meet orders, they had to resort to methods close to mass production. The Civil War gave the market to England, whose builders improved on the American designs.

The clipper could last only as long as the shipwright's customers distrusted steam; wind power, no matter how artfully captured, could not outrace engine power. In 1859, England's Royal School of Naval Architecture and Marine Engineering opened; it trained enginebuilders as well as ship designers. Isambard Kingdom Brunel's steamship *Great Eastern* was launched the same year; 690 feet long and weighing 19,000 tons, it was the largest ship yet seen. Brunel's backers went bankrupt, yet the *Great Eastern* proved itself in the laying of telegraphic cables along the ocean floor, connecting England with America.

Gradually, technical breakthroughs and public familiarity allowed the steam engine to come into its own. By 1875, passengers could cross the Atlantic by ocean liner in seven days. In 1877, the Lloyd's Register of Shipping set rules for acceptable steelwork; now not only iron but also its superior, steel, had been accepted as a shipbuilding material. Sail and wood gave way to steam and metal.

Shipwrights had worked with wood for thousands of years. They did not have the first idea how to make anything, including a ship, out of steel. On the other hand, Brunel, builder of the *Great Eastern*, had been trained as a civil engineer. With the coming of steam power, the companies that built engines took over the building of ships. Boilermakers, metalsmiths, and steam fitters became dockyard workers.

From 1895 to 1914, the tonnage of the Western nations' combined fleets rose from 17 million to 43 million. Once a ship passed a certain length, its size alone drove it faster through the water. The monsters of the 20th century dwarfed the *Great Eastern*. Germany's *Vaterland* was 904 feet long and weighed 54,000 tons. The French *Normandie*, launched in 1935, set the record; it weighed 79,280 tons and once sailed across the Atlantic in four days, three hours, and two minutes. In recent decades, most overseas passenger travel has gone by air, not by sea, but innovations have been made in cargo ships—most notably the *container ship* introduced after World War II. In these ships, cargo is stored in standard-sized containers, and the ship's hull is designed with these containers in mind. Loading and unloading is done by machine; the dock crew is stripped down to a tiny number. *Tankers* are designed with holds made up of a system of connected, uniform tanks. They carry liquids, oil being the most precious; the Universe line of tankers, built in Japan, can carry 326,000 tons each.

The 20th-century shipyard is a vast complex. Welders, blacksmiths, plumbers, carpenters, and electricians all work there; building a ship is much like putting together an office building all made of steel. Each shipyard is managed by a board of directors with a chairman at its head. The most important departments are those for production control, cost estimating, naval design, and overseeing the work until the ship is launched. Then the *outside finishing* department takes over, doing all the fitting-out required after the ship is afloat. The shipbuilders also hire subcontractors for the ship's engines and other machinery.

The *berth* is now used only as the point where the ship is assembled and from which the ship is launched; the ship itself is not built from scratch on the spot. The components are fashioned in separate foundaries; some shipyards simply receive prefabricated components from factories and then fit them together. *Drydock* shipyards are basins where the parts of a ship may be lowered into place by crane rather than lifted by men.

Shipbuilding apprentices in England are trained by dockyard schools under the Royal Navy. The schools teach physics and advanced mathematics and have standards that might have pleased William Sutherland, the 18th-century advocate of scientific shipbuilding. A quarter of the apprentices drop out after one year; after four years, graduates take examinations for admittance to the Royal Navy College at Greenwich. Those accepted are known as Naval Construction Cadets. Instruction at the College lasts three years; after graduating, cadets may join the Royal Corps of Naval Construction Cadets, designers of the country's warships. Those who drop out along the way become, depending on their degree of training, relatively well-paid shipyard craftsmen. No such system of training exists outside the military.

Elsewhere, civilian ship designers study for graduate degrees in the science as part of their higher education at universities or polytechnical schools. The designers are not formally known as *naval architects*. Employed by dockyards, they work from orders that stipulate at least the weight the ship should be able to carry, the speeds desired, and the number of people to travel on board. Different designs are also needed for different kinds of cargo, as with the container and tanker ships. Using training in physics, fluid mechanics, calculus, and other disciplines, the naval architect designs a ship that will meet each of the client's requirements. Like their land counterparts, naval architects do their chief work on paper; putting the ship together is not their responsibility. But they must have worked in a shipyard to understand the methods and materials that can be employed.

With the rise of modern steel leviathans, the woodworking shipwright became an endangered species. But some few shipwrights survive, keeping alive the old skills by building modern versions of the great sailing ships, often for individuals and groups themselves intent on preserving what they regard as the romantic past.

For related occupations in this volume, *Builders*, see the following:
Architects and Contractors

Carpenters
Construction Laborers
Plasterers and Other Finishing Workers
Plumbers

For related occupations in other volumes of the series, see the following:
in *Artists and Artisans* (to be published Fall 1986):):
  Glassblowers
in *Harvesters* (to be published Spring 1987):
  Whalers
in *Manufacturers and Miners* (to be published Fall 1987):
  Metalsmiths
  Power and Fuel Merchants
in *Warriors and Adventurers* (to be published Spring 1988):
  Sailors

Tunnelers and Blasters

Historically, *tunnelers* have been most closely associated with the transportation and mining industries. Ancient laborers (usually slaves) built tunnels underground, through mountains, and sometimes under narrow waterways so that pipe could be laid or other conduits built to bring water from springs into cities. The Romans were particularly adept at tunneling, but even as early as 2180 B.C.-2160 B.C. the Babylonians had built a brick-lined pedestrian tunnel 300 feet long beneath the Euphrates River, connecting the Royal Palace to the temple. In 41 A.D. the Romans used 30,000 laborers over a 10-year period to build a 3.5-mile tunnel to drain Lake Fucinus. Tunnelers also worked to build both horizontal and vertical shafts for mining purposes, and there was actually little differentiation made between tunnelers and *miners* for many centuries.

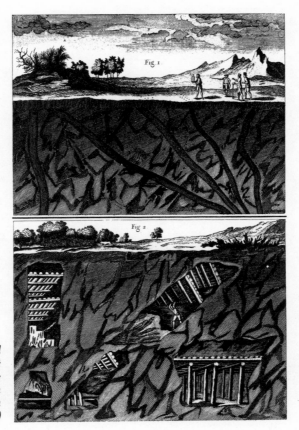

Tunnelers have always worked closely with miners, carving out avenues for mining and shoring them up with timbers. (From Diderot's Encyclopedia, late 18th century)

As mining became an important industry in the Middle Ages and later, tunneling became more sophisticated. In both East and West, solid rock was typically broken up through a method known as *fire-quenching*. A fire (usually underground) was burned furiously at the spot that was to be worked. When it reached its greatest intensity and the rock wall was red hot, cold water was poured on the rock, quenching the fire, and cracking the rock so that a pick and axe could more readily enter its surface.

Explosives—used in mines from the 11th century in China—began to be employed in Europe in the 17th century. Specialist *blasters* learned to use explosives to help open up the earth, not only for tunnelers and miners but also for *well-diggers* and *drillers*. Being responsible for the preparation, placement, and detonation of explosives, blasters gradually became highly trained in determining the necessary strength and pattern of a projected blast, as well as the amount, type, and location of explosive charge to be employed.

Black powder was a well-known explosive used in ancient China long before the Christian era, but it was not used in Europe until the 13th century A.D. In the 17th century, as transportation became more important in the commercially revived Western world, explosives began to be used in tunneling. When the Industrial Revolution began, both mining and transportation became essential ingredients of the new economic activity.

As early as 1681, when the Canal du Midi was completed in France, connecting the Atlantic Ocean and the Mediterranean Sea, canal-building became an important occupation of tunnelers. Miners were sometimes employed to work on canals as well as mine shafts, as was the case in 1761 when the Bridgewater Canal Tunnel was built so that coal could be cheaply and readily shipped from the Worsley mine to Manchester, England.

Canal-building flourished in the early 19th century, just before railroads emerged as the favored means of bulk transportation. Tunnelers also worked along with railroad builders; the first United States railroad tunnel was built between 1831 and 1833. Soon, canal activity all but ceased, but tunnelers were called upon for new underground work—the building of underwater tunnels. This was an extremely dangerous occupation, offering better than average pay to those who dared do it. In the first half of the 19th century, only a protective steel or iron shield separated tunnelers from the possible fatal rush of waters pressing down into the project site. Poisonous gas fumes also posed a health and safety hazard. Twenty tunnelers were killed in 1880 while building a pathway beneath the Hudson River. In 1908, a 25-man crew was killed by a sudden inflow of water at their tunnel site at Lotschberg in the Alps.

Tunneling methods were gradually improved by the use of explosives, power drills, dynamite, and steam power. Underwater tunnels are now constructed chiefly through the immersed-tube technique; above-water machinery digs into riverbeds, and huge tubes are then sunk into the cavities, which are finally refilled and sealed. This method is obviously much safer than the old ways. Tunneling today is a skilled and mechanized occupation. *Engineers* and *machine operators* are well trained for their jobs, and they command a good salary. The industry is also much less labor-intensive than in the past; because of the improvement in techniques and machines, fewer jobs are available in the profession than there were in the previous century. There are still a fair amount of dirty, back-breaking jobs related to tunneling, however. These are filled by common laborers called *sandhogs*, who earn much less money than workers in positions requiring technical and mechanical skills.

The hiring of professional blasters became common in the latter part of the 19th century. In 1846 nitroglycerin was discovered in Italy, and similar explosives were soon developed in Germany. The most important changes came in the 1860's when the Swedish *chemist* Alfred Bernhard Nobel developed dynamite, shortly after he had devised the blasting cap to house chemical initiators for charge detonation. Dynamite was the explosive most

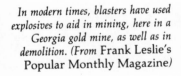

In modern times, blasters have used explosives to aid in mining, here in a Georgia gold mine, as well as in demolition. (From Frank Leslie's Popular Monthly Magazine*)*

commonly used by blasters before World War II. During the war many blasters were used by military forces to set covert explosive mines.

Blasters' work can be separated into stages: drilling holes in patterns; placing charges and detonators in each; tamping and stemming the charge to compact the explosive; detonating the charge; and clearing the blasted area. Some workers specialize in certain aspects of blasting. *Power loaders* fill blast holes with charge; *dumper-bailer operators* dump sand and cement over charges, using special bailers and hoists; *shooters* detonate torpedoes in bored oil or gas wells in order to initiate or renew the flow of precious fuels. Most recently, some blasters have refined the technique of building demolition through charge detonation. These *demolition engineers* are able to bring down huge skyscrapers into a uniform heap in an instant, without damaging other structures standing right beside them. It is a task requiring considerable skill, precision, and engineering knowledge.

Suggestions for Further Reading

For further information about builders, you may wish to consult the books below.

General

Briggs, Martin S. *A Short History of the Building Crafts*. London: Oxford University Press, 1925. Contains useful information on carpenters from all periods.

Gimpel, Jean. *The Cathedral Builders*, translated by Carl F. Barnes, Jr. London: Evergreen Books, 1961. On the medieval master-builders and the craftspeople who worked under them.

Jones, Gwilym Peredur. "Building in Stone in Medieval Western Europe." *The Cambridge Economic History of Europe*, Vol. 2, *Trade and Industry in the Middle Ages*. M. Postan and E.E. Rich, eds. Cambridge: Cambridge University Press, 1952. A very useful general essay on the life and work of medieval builders.

Needham, Joseph, with Wang Ling and Lu Gwei-Djen. *Science and Civilization in China, Vol.4: Physics and Physical Technology, Part 3: Civil Engineering and Nautics*. Cambridge: At the University Press, 1971. Part of a modern classic series, with much detail on techniques and practices, and illustrations of builders at work.

Stockham, Peter, ed. *Little Book of Early American Crafts and Trade*. New York: Dover Publications, 1976. Excerpts from *The Book of Trades*, an 1804 reference book about craftspeople and their work.

Architects and Contractors

Brill, Martin S. *The Architect in History*. Oxford: Oxford University Press, 1927. An invaluable review of the life and practice of the Western architect, from ancient Greece to Victorian England.

Dixon, Roger, and Stefan Muthesius. *Victorian Architecture*. New York: Oxford University Press, 1978.

Hamlin, Talbot. *Architecture Through the Ages*, revised edition. New York: Putnam, 1953. A useful standard review.

Harvey, John. *The Master Builders: Architecture in the Middle Ages*. New York: McGraw-Hill, 1971. A small book that is enlightening on methods, building styles, and historical backgrounds; pays attention to the working mason as well as the designer.

Kinross, Lord. *Hagia Sophia: A History of Constantinople*. New York: Newsweek, 1979. On the Byzantine church, its place in history, and its building; includes color photographs and reproductions.

Kostoff, Spiro, ed. *The Architect: Chapters in the History of the Profession*. New York: Oxford University Press, 1977. A collection of original essays describing the rise of the architect, from ancient Egypt to today.

Lux, Donald G., Willis E. Ray, and A. Dean Havenstein. *The World of Construction*. Bloomington, Ill.: McKnight & McKnight, 1970. A textbook on building procedures and the industry's operation.

Mayer, L.A. *Islamic Architects and Their Works*. Geneva: Albert Kundig, 1956. A historical catalogue, with an introduction on the Islamic architects' status.

United Nations Educational, Scientific and Cultural Organization (UNESCO). *Preserving and Restoring Monuments and Historic Buildings*. Paris: UNESCO, 1972. On the aims, administration, and methods of architectural restoration, with present-day examples and brief historical background.

Carpenters

Bowyer, Jack. *History of Building*. London: Crosby Lockwood Staples, 1973.

Bridenbaugh, Carl. *Cities in Revolt: Urban Life in America 1743-1776*. New York: Knopf, 1968. On Colonial carpenters and the part they played in city life.

———. *The Colonial Craftsman*. New York: New York University Press, 1950. Contains information on many craftspeople, including the pay and status of the 18th-century carpenter.

Feirer, John, and Gilbert Hutchings. *Carpentry and Building Construction*. Peoria, Ill.: Chas. A. Bennett, 1976. On the state and practice of the industry today.

Kingsford, Peter. *Builders and Building Workers*. London: Edward Arnold, 1973. On the plight of English carpenters in the 19th century.

Oliveira Marques, A. H. de. *Daily Life in Portugal in the Late Middle Ages*. Madison, Wis.: University of Wisconsin Press, 1971. Includes information on medieval carpenters' pay and practices.

Russell, Loris. *Everyday Life in Colonial Canada*. London: B.T. Batsford, 1973. Contains information on the building of log cabins.

Construction Laborers

Barber, G. *Builders' Plant and Equipment*. London: Newnes- Butterworths, 1973. A guide to modern equipment, with a brief history in the first chapter.

Cherry, Mike. *Steel Beams and Iron Men*. New York: Four Winds Press, 1980. An ironworker turned writer tells of his experiences; includes many photographs.

Masons

Bagley, J.J. *Life in Medieval England*. New York: Putnam, 1967. Includes a chapter on the building and decoration of churches.

Benson, Elizabeth P. *The Maya World*. New York: Thomas Y. Crowell, 1977.

Knoop, Douglas, and G.P. Jones. *The London Mason in the 17th Century*. London: Manchester University Press, 1935. On the operation of the mason's trade, based on documents from the time.

Rowling, Marjorie. *Everyday Life in Medieval Times*. New York: Putnam, 1968. Includes a chapter on church builders and artists.

White, Jon Manchip. *Everyday Life in Ancient Egypt*. New York: Putnam, 1963. Contains sections on masons and the building of the pyramids.

Plasterers

Bankart, George Parcy. *The Art of the Plasterer*. London: B.T. Batsford, 1908. The title continues: "the decorative development of the craft, chiefly in England from the XVIth to the XVIIIth century; with chapters on...the classic period and...the Italian Renaissance."

Millar, William. *Plastering Plain and Decorative*. London: B.T. Batsford, 1897. The title continues: "A Practical Treatise...Together with an account of historical plastering in England, Scotland, and Ireland." The introduction by G.T. Robinson, "A Glimpse of its History," is an anecdotal view from the Greeks onward.

Plumbers

Blankenbaker, E. Keith. *Modern Plumbing*. South Holland, Ill.: Goodheart-Willcox, 1978. A vocational guide and technical manual.

Gerhard, William Paul. "A Half-Century of Sanitation: 1850-1899." *American Architect*, Feb. 25, March 4, and

March 11, 1899. "A Paper read at the meeting of the Brooklyn Engineers' Club, February 9, 1899," by a sanitary engineer.

Leeds, Albert R. *Recent Progress in Sanitary Science.* Salem, Mass.: Salem Press, 1877. An address delivered to the Lyceum of Natural History, New York.

Wright, Lawrence. *Clean and Decent.* London: Routledge & Kegan Paul, 1960. On plumbing through history, in the United States, France, and, especially, England.

Shipwrights

Abell, Sir Westcott. *The Shipwright's Trade.* Cambridge: Cambridge University Press, 1948. A technical history of English shipbuilding.

Casson, Lionel. *Ships and Seamanship in the Ancient World.* Princeton, N.J.: Princeton University Press, 1971. On kinds of ships and shipbuilding techniques, in detail.

Goldenberg, Joseph A. *Shipbuilding in Colonial America.* Charlottesville, Va.: University Press of Virginia, 1976. Includes a chapter on Colonial shipwrights, their training, work, and status.

Laing, Alexander. *American Ships.* New York: American Heritage Press, 1977. Includes a chapter on the kayak and the umiak; the rest of the book follows American ship construction to present-day whalers.

Torr, Cecil. *Ancient Ships.* Chicago: Argonaut, 1964; a reprint of the 1894 edition. A classic work, including a modern appendix on Greek ships.

INDEX

104, 107
Truck drivers, 66
Trucking industry, 133
Tunnelers, x, 161-65
Tunnels, 6, 120, 126, 161;
    underwater, 163-64
Turners, 47
Turnpike trusts, 129, 131,
    133
Turnpikes, 129

Udine, Gionnide, 101
Umiaks, 148
Ummani, 122
Under the Greenwood Tree
    (Hardy), 92-93
Unionization, 54
Unions, 53, 56, 93, 103,
    117-18
United Association of
    Journeymen and
    Apprentices of the
    Plumbers and Pipefitters
    Industry of the United
    States and Canada, 118
United Nations Educational,
    Scientific, and Cultural
    Organization, 36
United States: architects,
    architecture, 32-33, 34,
    35; carpentry, 55-56;
    masons, 96; operational
    engineers, 66-67;
    plasterers, 104; public
    waterworks, 114; roads,
    roadbuilding, 132-33;
    shipwrights, 156
Universal equipment

operators, 66
Universe tankers, 157
University of Glascow, 28

Vasari, Giacomo, 20, 22,
    102
Vaterland (ship), 157
Vatican: Loggia, 101
Vaulting, 16
Verrocchio (architect), 22
Via Appia (Appian Way), 123
Viae publicae, 123
Viae vicinales, 123
Victoria, queen of England,
    28
Vikings, 142-43
Vinci, Leonardo da, 21
Virginia, 91
Vitruvius, 8, 13;
    Architecture, 64, 99

Wages. See Pay (wages)
Wagons, 128, 130, 133
Wallpaper, 104
Walls, 78, 91, 95, 112
Warehouses, 27
Warlords, 44-45
Wars, 16, 120
Warships, 140, 158
Waste disposal, 109-10,
    111, 113-14
Water power, 53, 64
Water supply, public, 109,
    111
Water systems, 27, 109,
    111-12, 113, 114, 117
Waterworks, 6, 114

Weavers, 20
Wedges, 44, 75, 82
Welders, 157
Well-diggers, 91, 162
West: architecture in, 13-
    24
Western Asia, 12
Westminster Abbey, 13
Westminster Hall, 46
Wheeled vehicles, 133
Whetstone, 46
Whitewashers, 100
William of Colchester, 86
Wind power, 27, 156
Windsor Palace, 112
Wire rope, 63-64
Women, 34, 47, 56, 69, 102
Wood, x-xi, 11; as building
    material, 39-40, 42, 45,
    46, 47, 76, 81; in
    shipbuilding, 139, 143,
    152, 156
Wood crafts, 52
Woodworking, xi
Woolworth Tower, 67
Wooton, "Uncle" Richard,
    133
Workshops, 53-54, 89
Worshipful Company of
    Carpenters, 47
Wyatt, James, 35

Yakushi-ji Construction
    Agency, 11-12
York Cathedral, 18
York Minster, 85, 86

Zoroastrians, 109